MY LIVES

MY LIVES

ROSEANNE ARNOLD

BALLANTINE BOOKS · NEW YORK

Grateful acknowledgment is made to the following for
permission to reprint previously published material:

BEYOND WORDS PUBLISHING, INC. AND WILLIAM MORRIS AGENCY, INC:
"Autobiography in Five Short Chapters" from *There's a Hole in My
Sidewalk* by Portia Nelson, copyright © 1977 by Portia Nelson.
Reprinted by permission.

PATTI SMITH:
Lyrics excerpt from the song "People Have the Power" by Fred Smith
and Patti Smith. Reprinted by permission.

THE NEW YORK TIMES:
Excerpt from "What Am I Anyway, a Zoo?" by Roseanne Arnold,
originally appeared as an Op-Ed on July 31, 1989. Copyright © 1989
by The New York Times Company. Reprinted by permission.

Certain photographs are reprinted courtesy of Don Cadette/Viacom,
appearing in the following order: nos. 8, 9, 10, 11, 13, 14, 15, 17.
Photographs appearing in the following order, nos. 1, 2, 3, 4, 5, 6, 7,
12, 16, 18, and 19, are courtesy of Roseanne Arnold.

ISBN 0-346-37815-6

Design by Holly Johnson

Manufactured in the United States of America

For Tom

I am a small green vine wrapping
around you, as the wind shakes me
and the rain bruises my head.

You and I are our own garden.
Unpruned, unmarked, we drink
and grow, gnarled in elemental magic.

I feed you and am nurtured.
The black earth in whom you sit
envelops me as
I float through you,
My love.

You are blooming and fragrant.

ACKNOWLEDGMENTS

I'd like to thank Michael Angeli, who became a good friend of mine during the life of this book. I had incredible trouble with the sequence of events in my life, and never wanting to understand sequential or "logical" thinking, because I perceive it to be wholly male-defined and inflicted, I just hired a *MALE* to help me with it. Aside from his inborn and genetic thought patterns, Michael was invaluable in contribution, and talent.

Thank you also to:
My doctors
Phoebe Snow
Anne
Antoinette
The Troops for Truddi Chase
Kari
Marilyn and Larry Atler
My kids
Laurie, Erin, Mary
Kim, Julie, and Terry
My dolls

CONTENTS

AUTOBIOGRAPHY IN FIVE SHORT CHAPTERS

Chapter I

I walk, down the street.
There is a deep hole in the sidewalk.
I fall in.
I am lost . . . I am helpless.
It isn't my fault.
It takes forever to find a way out.

Chapter II

I walk down the same street.
There is a deep hole in the sidewalk.
I *pretend* I don't see it.
I fall in again.
I can't believe I am in the same place.
But it isn't my fault.
It still takes a long time to get out.

Chapter III

I walk down the same street.
There is a deep hole in the sidewalk.
I see it is there.
I still fall in . . . it's a habit . . . but,
my eyes are open.
I know where I am.
It is *my* fault.
I get out immediately.

Chapter IV

I walk down the same street.
There is a deep hole in the sidewalk.
I walk around it.

Chapter V

I walk down another street.

—Portia Nelson

P R E F A C E

So I was, like, Jesus, Jesus, I'm really gonna do this, I'm really gonna make it. Make it out, make it out alive, make it big, make money, make it over the rainbow, make all my dreams come true.

And when I took that stage, I had earned it, it was mine. I took the two steps up and was transported into another world, another realm of being, Standing Up, Standing There, and the pain and the truth and the fear just rolled off me like sweat does, beading around my lips and running into my eyes, leaving me jacked and worn and almost limp, 'cause at last my life had all just become a story and I had that story to tell and to sell, and I was gonna get rich. Rich as Eddie Murphy, Bill Cosby, Richard Pryor, Bette Midler, all of them. I was taking that same little magic plywood box with a mike attached all the way to where? The top?

All of my little life I wanted to be a "star," to get out, rise above, transcend, shine, burn. I was twenty-eight now and had found that stage, that vehicle to transport me away from a sad, frightening, colored childhood that did not seem, somehow, to belong to me.

I always knew I was different. My little friends at school were not or seemed not to be obsessed with hiding and saving themselves and forgetting always where they were and what day it was.

Even at the age when I ran and played and at an age

where each tooth is even and barely hanging beneath the gum line and not even thinking about being loose, even then I couldn't remember.

The reason I didn't remember for a very long time is simple. The parts of me that knew everything, the parts that recorded and filed and remembered had each split off, became its own being, its own story, its own country.

I always went away to the place right at the top of my head. I could make my eyes look straight up through the sockets of the skull and see clearly into outer space, the other world, the world beyond. Everything below was blotted out into insignificance. It was all revolving, yet empty, and meant nothing. It was just a test, making me stronger and stronger, the more numb I could make myself.

I thought I was becoming a saint of sorts, like Joan of Arc, or even Jesus, who also had to suffer because of the ignorance of less evolved humans.

When I went away, I left my body completely and could hear other voices all around me chattering about how God would make me strong and how nobody could really "get" me. A spiritual message, really, as if a strong part of me would reach God and be comforted.

Because I had to go away so often and so fully, other parts had to be invented and grafted on. Those parts took care of the everyday chores, the work, the explaining, the covering, the keeping of Time.

Each one had its own function in the system, this

perfectly timed and carefully synchronized system of inner community.

There are children in here, too, many children—all wounded, broken, damaged, and flapping heavy wings, unable to rise. There are both boys and girls, men and women, mortals and gods, heretics and hysterics, there are poets and killers and bigots as well as saints.

Now you have met the major characters in our story. There are also many more, not all of whom can speak yet. All parts will weave in and out, which is how we have always lived and still do. We will give you our names when it becomes necessary.

I am Woman Hear Me Roar. At least, I *do* roar, and refuse to whimper. I roar like the old shopping-bag ladies at the various bus stops in the various dead hearts of the various dying cities where nothing makes any noise because they're suffocating on their own puke. I roar like the victim whose throat has been cut and no vocal chords chime, only the lips open and close in some rhythm approximating speech. I roar like the trees bent over and gnarled, flinging themselves backward against the attacking wind like the helpless victims that God created them to be. I roar inside my skin, branded.

I used to think victim meant woman. Woman is what victims turn into, I think now, laughing ironically, and making this period (.) Even the men.

Every child is Jesus Saint Joan of Arc, getting the perfection and the beauty kicked out and delivered to the cross, the pyre by those they came to save. In elevating distress, there are many voices that speak each day with veiled eyes and whispers.

Many is the name we were given. Darkness is the path we explore. Empty is the face of the vessel that waits for restoration near the shore.

MY LIVES

THE SHOW
MUST BEGIN

The one who cares the most wins. That's what I read in *The Art of War*, that two-thousand-year-old book by some Oriental wise man that everyone in Hollywood owns.

That's how I knew I'd end up with everyone else waving the white flags and not me. That's how I knew I'd be the last person standing when it was all over. They don't call me queen of the closers for nothing. I cared the most.

I may have underestimated the "wins" part. In the

end, you couldn't measure what I had won unless you had a scale or a tape measure calibrated in light-years.

This particular war was a bitch, a load, a heavy metal dinosaur, a honker of a thing, my friend, called "Roseanne."

Once upon a time in a land far, far, far away, a land of dreams and imagination, below time and space . . .

TV producers Marcy Carsey and Tom Werner liked their people to feel special, unfortunately sometimes for the same, mutually exclusive reasons another person felt special. It was 1987. Carsey and Werner wanted me to meet with this hot Young Turk named Matt Williams; he was their choice as head writer for "Roseanne." I was told that "Roseanne" was *my* show and that Matt was *my* head writer. Marcy and Tom told Matt that it was *his* show and that *I* was *his* star. Naturally, we both thought we were sitting on top of the world when it was just a one-seater.

Matt Williams. Another sensitive, white male Anglo-Saxon Protestant, lavished with praise because he could write for TV, *the woman's media* (in lieu of actually hiring a woman to do it). He was as scared as I was, and we were both trying to get what bit of the brass ring we could get. According to Carsey-Werner, Matt was the best pure writer they had. He'd been script supervisor for "The Cosby Show" and wrote the pilot for

"A Different World." This had to be overkill as far as I was concerned. All I needed was a collaborator, someone to get everything on paper, because every idea was mine.

After four months of so-called collaboration—me going to New York to work with him, Matt coming to my house, along with enough telephone calls to keep AT&T solvent for the next ten years, Matt turned in his first version of what was to be the "Roseanne" show pilot. I read it and my God, I just flipped. Jackie's character (played by Laurie Metcalf), which was the sister, was me. My character was totally passive, like just about every other woman on TV. Functionally, I may as well have been a pin-setter or the lady who hands the knife thrower his daggers. My character spent most of her time sitting in the corner like a stump, saying "And then what happened? And then what happened?" June Cleaver was Patty Hearst compared to this character. I was not "Roseanne" and it wasn't pretty. I took a meeting with Marcy Carsey and Tom Werner, with Matt Williams sitting in for ballast.

"How did this happen? The sister's *my* character!" I screamed. I have since learned to pace myself because there's nothing like starting a discussion off at full bore to get you written off as insane and hysterical.*

"Well," Matt spoke indolently, like a pampered rich

_____

*Women take note.

kid, "I just didn't think people would like you as the main character."

"So you're telling me what I did for the last six years, in fact the very thing that got me this show, I did really well just so I could give it to someone else? Then I quit. I'm not gonna give away my character after it took my whole goddamn life to build it. I'M NOT DOING IT."

This was my first clue into the warped mind and language of Hollywood. This was the first of many times that reality has grabbed my head and wrenched it until it slams and spins and stops, horrified. Speaking of the "main character," Matt would say, "*She* wouldn't do that." I'd stare, open-mouthed, for a few minutes.

"She who?"

"Roseanne," he'd answer, as though I'd asked him who was buried in Bud Abbott's tomb.

"*She* would do that, Matt, and you know how I know she would? Because *I'm* she, you dumb bastard."

"Not you, Roseanne, the person," he'd laugh, "Roseanne, the character." Once again, Matt lectured me about what would work "dramatically." Or, drawing on some other 101 college writing course horseshit Matt was expert on: "But Roseanne the character is just a condensed version of Roseanne-the-human-being, okay? Not dramatically, Roseanne," he'd pontificate.

I don't know where else on earth people speak in this way. "AHHH!!" I remarked.

"Oh, you'll calm down, and you'll be able to work with Matt." Marcy tried to defuse the situation by not only giving her words a kind of foretelling tone, but subtly putting them in the form of a command. And I did just that—I worked with Matt, which now seems as improbable as a meteor shower, but work with him I did. And the more we worked, the more ridiculous it got. After scrapping the first draft, Matt, in rapid succession, turned my show into the little boy's story (told from a child's point of view) and then the Dad's (witness "Home Improvement," which he likewise "created"). He could not get it into his head that a woman was the main character and that she was *not passive*. He couldn't understand that the female character could *drive* scenes, that the family functioned *because* of her, not in spite of her. I gave him books on feminist theory, talked into tape recorders for hours, lectured him on motherhood and matriarchy for hours and hours, but he just never caught on.

After Matt's second draft blew chunks, I rewrote it, rewrote every scene, taking stuff from my act, wrote the sister's part, punched up the daughter's part. (Once again, in a pivotal scene, Matt wanted the son to be the driving force—he didn't get it that I wanted a totally *female-driven show.*)

This is, after all, the thing I came to Hollywood to do, as well as for "Art" itself. Feeling bitter and tired of the constant insult to my gender in all forms of media, the unabated whining of male ego and thought as it regards my sex, I wanted to give the gander a bit of what he'd been giving the goose for *eons* now.

Separating the wheat from the chaff is hard to do when you are attempting to make a general statement using only personal knowledge. So, there were actually two simultaneous things going on: (1) My "Art" and (2) My Real Life. I don't really know yet which one imitated which, where they intersected, paralleled, or canceled each other out.

I wanted to create a real woman/mother on TV—for political reasons, as an activist. I wanted to hear/see a world-weary, pop-culture-hating woman whose complaint was timeless and purely female: "I create and feed the world, and I do it for millennia to my own exclusion and demise." (Talk about your Catch-22! When Freud said women's nature was masochistic, he forgot to notice that men psychiatrists tend to blame their lack of political sophistication on women's biology.)

Males have a very hard time seeing outside themselves. Generally, they lack the wisdom and vision to include themselves in the world of women. It is my humble opinion that this is why they should stay home.

Anyway, I always assumed that the show would be created by Matt Williams and Roseanne Barr. After I had rewritten all those scenes and we had filmed the pilot, I was invited to see it. When the credits rolled, it said "Created by Matt Williams." And that was all. I felt robbed and began to wail. Someone recently asked me how such a thing could happen. The answer is simply because it can and it does every day in Hollywood.

"You get me that created-by credit," I pressed my manager, Arlyne Rothberg. "This show is based on my kids, our life, and me. No one's gonna take credit for my work." I was burning up, and what's worse, the whole damn thing would rise up again and again, like vines on a jungle path, always strangling, obliterating, halting my advance. Because everyone is always claiming *they* created me. Relatives, sisters, managers, writers, executives, ex-husbands, the postman, the milkman, hell, the guy selling oranges from a shopping basket on the corner probably thinks he did, too. They sue me, I give them money, and managers, agents, and producers grow fatter and fatter off of my sweat. People don't think right out here.

"Please—you gotta help me get my 'created-by' credit." I made this last, misbegotten overture not to my agent, not to my manager, or even God Almighty, but to the one guy, fellow writer, collaborator, all around good guy—Matt Williams.

"I will help you," he promised. "And I will call the Writers Guild, and we'll get this right." The evolutionary upright walk of compassion lasted until that same night. When Matt called the Writers Guild, he did the opposite and told them that his star was out of control, that she had a huge ego and wanted credit where credit wasn't due. Suddenly, we were all apes again. This was told to me by a low-level woman (of course) who heard the call at the Writers Guild. Us low-level gals could stop the world if we ever get organized.

"There'll come a day when you'll be really pissed that you let that go," I told comedian Tim Allen a few years ago. The same thing had happened to him with his show, which was literally based on his comedy act. Who got creative credit for Tim Allen's show? Matt Williams.

Okay. I didn't get creative credit, and I was devastated by it, very disappointed and royally butt-packed. I was getting screwed. It made no sense. My poor head was spinning like a hurricane.

I felt so low that I *really* started to get high. I started smoking pot on weekends with my husband. For a short while it was just two tokes, always in control, in case the kids cut themselves and we had to take them to the hospital or something. Gradually, I worked my way into the cheap days until I was a full-fledged hemp-hustling reefer queen. Drugs and food seemed a way of dealing with the frustration. It was horrible, helpless frustration, black frustration, pure white frustration, loud frustration, speechless frustration, unrelenting frustration—complete frustration.

This was not the best time of my life, and surely it should've been. My whole goddamn life was coming apart like a cheap Halloween costume. My kids were completely out of control, while I was working fifteen hours a day plus weekends. I screamed a lot, something

I'm not particularly proud of, but it was that or firearms.
I screamed at the beginning, in the middle, as a first resort, as a last resort, as a matter of fact. And now, in the
end, I write a book.

We went on to shoot episodes, sort of the way chick-
ens continue to run after they've been beheaded.

The second episode of the series had me totally
psyched. After much argument and revision, the point of
view of this episode was at last in keeping with the vision
of the pilot, about the remarkable courage of the ordinary American working woman. There was a scene
where "Roseanne" and an older waitress drink a toast to
all the working women everywhere. I was amped to perform it, and was screwing around, having fun and getting
myself up. In those days, we did two shows in front of a
live audience on tape day.

I was new to the form of TV and was using the first
show as sort of a dress rehearsal, not giving it everything
I could because I was used to doing an early show and a
late show. And comics usually "save it for the end."

Instead of calling me aside and telling me I should
get my shit together and do better, or asking what my
problem was (like any decent producer or director who
had already surpassed me by two years in TV experience), Matt called the entire cast, including extras and
children, upstairs into the makeup room. Doing his best
Robert De Niro impression (acting had been his first
choice in show biz), he silently stalked the room, back

and forth for a while. Then, stopping cold dead in the middle of us all, he said with much disgust that "the show tonight is not working." And then, coming closer and closer to me, until our noses almost touched, he screamed, "AND IT'S ALL YOUR FAULT!!!!!!"

Everyone flinched, as I squirmed uncomfortably in my chair, but I didn't take my eyes off him. Steam was coming out from my bowels, and I wanted to blow him away. I was good at taking humiliation in my real life then. Thing is, he didn't realize, nor did I yet, that this show-biz world was not part of my real life. It had been invented to supersede my real life; I was fighting for *all* women here, not just my own pitiful self. I was making a STATEMENT. And I needed to believe that people who are making statements are above the law and above humiliation.

I swallowed hard and did a show right after that. I must admit that that is the episode I cannot ever watch because too much of my bravura looked threadbare and the fear shows through. I had been put in my place and started to think that I would lose everything I had worked for if I did not just do what he wanted me to do. (This tactic has been used on me countless times by producers and ABC executives, by the way.) I tried hard to do that. My resolve, however, dissolved after about two weeks. Was it because I was so headstrong or because I was so self-destructive? How can I really answer that question, knowing that, in the end, every woman who is headstrong is called self-destructive anyway?

Matt had written this scene where this dumb slob of a friend of Dan's comes in the kitchen while I'm making dinner. In the scene, this "MAN" spits a big lunger into my sink. For those first episodes, Matt must've got his inspiration by hanging out in airport bathrooms during flu season. There was just a ton of snot and shit jokes, stuff you'll never see on my show now because I hate that stuff. When the gob joke came, I flipped out.

"NOBODY'S GONNA SPIT IN MY FUCKING SINK!" I screamed. The line wasn't in the script either, so everyone knew I had blown a gasket right there. I heard people whispering, "God, she's loony," stuff like that, with the backs of their hands to each other's ears. In that case, I was gonna get my money's worth out of this psychotic break. I got right into Matt's face, could've sucked out his will to live with my nostrils had I wanted to, that's how close I was. He seemed a little uncomfortable, shocked, taken aback by this unfeminine behavior in a girl.

"You can't write my show, Matt."

"Uh-huh." He waved me off, as though I was homeless and asked him for wine money.

"No, Matt. You cannot do it, you weak, fucking bastard. You lying prick. You hack son of a bitch, talentless bag of shit. Give me some fucking jokes, you asshole!" Male language worked like a charm on Matt, not because I was speaking a vernacular he understood, but because it just plain scared the daylights out of him. Women, as a point of reference for him, were the ones who *served coffee*, so he had no idea who or what I was. By now he was staring at me as if I needed a snake charmer to part my hair.

"As soon as I can, motherfucker, your ass is *out the door*, do you understand, Matt Williams? Because I'm gonna be here a long time after you."

Well, Matt did what he did best, which was to tattle and make lists, two qualities that would endear him with the Third Reich but make him a certifiable neurotic in real life and, worse, get him killed in prison. Matt went to the network and complained, then had his assistant producer keep a tally sheet of how often I belched and farted while I entertained the audiences between tapings. If he would've been really sharp he would've reported on the verbal content of my humor, which at the time was turning into a battle cry against the power structure that "Roseanne" was going to destroy. It went something like this: "Ladies and gentlemen, I'm glad you like the show, and you know, I really love doing it. There's just one thing I'd like to say to the producers and the network: Could you take the dick out of my ass one little inch? It hurts and I just can't dance as good as you want me to with it in there." This now seems good enough weaponry to have brought me down, but instead, Matt went running to the network with his farting list as proof of how "out of control" I was and tried to get me fired from my own show. After the third episode, John Goodman and Laurie Metcalf were asked to do the show without me— they refused. After I found out, I knocked on Matt's door.

"Hey—I know what you did. I know you're stealing all my work, you fucking bastard, and you'll pay for it, too. Don't think you're gonna get away with it because *you are not.*"

"Well, *you* know what?" Matt hissed back. "I don't even care. Anything it takes to see you fucking go down in flames and to see you *fucked*, I'm gonna do, and I don't care if I go down with ya!"*

Third episode: Matt had his list, so I went ahead and made out mine. At the top of the list, I wrote: THESE ARE THE PEOPLE I'M GOING TO FIRE AS SOON AS MY SHOW GOES TO NUMBER ONE. THESE ARE THE PEOPLE WHO WILL BE OUT OF HERE. CHECK TO SEE IF YOUR NAME APPEARS BELOW. The list was long and I didn't play any favorites—everyone, good or bad, was on the list. At the top was Brandon Stoddard, president of ABC at the time, who refused to aid me when I went to him for help.

"You were twenty-one when you signed that con-

---

*Matt instead signed a multimillion-dollar deal with Disney Productions for movies, TV, etc.

tract," he told me. That made him the headliner, followed by Carsey and Werner, Matt Williams, all of his peons, cronies, and jerk-offs. I also wrote down the names of anyone who made it worthwhile to drag my tired ass there every day, like John Goodman and Laurie Metcalf. All the bad people got a big fat check by their names. There were a few on the bubble, so to speak, people who could go either way. For these, I put "N/A," for "not applicable at this time," but watch out. Then I tacked the list on my door for everyone to see. Yeah, I had probably lost it by that time, should've been dragged out and shot like they did to Old Yeller when they found out he was rabid, but somehow, foaming at the mouth, eyes crossed, goddamn loony birds circling the top of my head, I hung on. By the end of the next season, all the people who'd been checked on the list were gone—they were all gone, including Brandon Stoddard. I did some heavy voodoo, I did some intense meditation, I did tricks with mirrors and candles and everything, talisman, chicken-foot ritual, bones rolling, spirit-summoning, step-on-a-crack, break-your-mother's-back thing I could think of because I was gonna win. I had to do a lot of ritual things to get myself to *know* that I cared the most.

By show four, Matt's unbridled resentment began to manifest itself in the writing, specifically through my lines. The more he hated me, the more he took it out on me in the script. The lines were so reactive and victimish for women—all castration jokes or silly-ass "war of the sexes" jokes—and I couldn't do them. My character was becoming not unlike a typical TV male pig. So I started changing lines in rehearsal to avoid playing this monster that Matt was trying to, what, expose? And I'd change the words into the most loving person, the most loving mother. For a while, he just bit his tongue because I did have approval of the scripts and the writers in my contract (which I wisely asked for, but in my own hubris, I didn't understand that asking for and getting approval had nothing on earth to do with THE LAST WORD, which belonged to someone else). In the time it takes for a mushroom to blossom on cow dung, we were having all-out hollering matches again. The shouting I could handle. What struck me as odd, though, was the occasional presence of Carsey and Werner on the set. They'd stand there with their arms around Matt while I, their star, who was gonna make them all their goddamn money, would be reduced to tears.

The shit had to, and did, hit the fan during one particular episode where I'm supposed to be in bed with John Goodman while we're having this minor tiff. My character is supposed to say, "Well, you're my equal in bed, but that's it."

"I'm not gonna say this line about 'you're my equal in bed,' " I objected. "That's a man's line. That is not in keeping with my character. That is not a woman's voice, and I'm not gonna say it."

"You will say it as written," Matt ordered. It was a

little like Martin Short doing a Charles Laughton line, but effective nonetheless. "You will say it as written," he repeated, while I just sat there.

"You say it as written," he demanded.

"I ain't gonna say it as written."

"YES, YOU ARE."

"Fuck you. I AIN'T. My character wouldn't say anything like that." I'd heard other actresses use this type of language before, and I suddenly found it useful.

"Yes your *character* would," Matt caught on.

"And I'm telling you right now, I'M TELLING YOU, ASSHOLE, that she wouldn't. I know this character. I know this character better than you know your oily little self."

Matt went back to the phone. About an hour later, I'm sitting there on the bed, with John Goodman next to me. The cameras are waiting to roll, and surrounding the bed are all of Carsey-Werner's lawyers, the network's lawyers and the lawyer's lawyers, waiting for me to say the line he wrote. I was told I was in breach of contract and that I was too out of control to remain on the show—unless, of course, I said the line.

"Now, please—say the line, Miss Barr," one of them requested in an even, nonconfrontational tone. Sure, it was just a line of dialogue, but now I know how all those prisoners of war felt when they were ordered to spit on the flag or face a firing squad. Problem was, for the life of me, I just couldn't work up a gob, and that line was

16

nothing more than a wad of spit anyway, so I just sat there on the bed.

"SAY THE GODDAMN LINE, ROSEANNE," someone else finally blurted out.

"Look, I'm not gonna say it. And I'm not gonna tell you again that I'm not gonna say it. You change the line. Or I will. I can lay here until moss starts to grow between my toes. I'm in bed. What do I care?" I looked around me, and people were observing me with the mournfulness you might have for a biology-class frog if you were having a vulnerable day.

The little bed-in went on for another twenty minutes until Ellen Falcon—this talentless, fat-assed bitch-*directoress* who roamed around on cement all day on high heels and obeyed Matt's orders—signaled and all the cameras went dark.

"That's it," she said, "we'll, uh . . . we'll do it to-morrow."

"Whatever . . . I'm goin' home," I said. I could've pissed hydrochloric acid, I was so mad. And going home didn't help because there I had my husband, Bill, talking in my ear, which was bad enough. I found out later, however, that he had Matt Williams's gnarly little ear, too. Bill had been calling him all along, telling him how crazy I was the whole time that I was trying to make a power move on the show. Bill wasn't stupid. He was dishonest, scheming, disloyal, and as big a coward that ever painted his ass black to hide in the night, but he wasn't stupid and, like everyone else, he thought he'd make out a lot better by siding with Matt.

The next day, I told all of them that I'd be in my trailer until they got the line change. I considered walking out, but thought better of it because I knew that the minute I did, they'd say I broke my contract and then get rid of me. So I spent the day in my trailer watching TV ("Oprah" and talk shows, nothing Carsey-Werner produced, incidentally). It was the following afternoon that the line change finally came down. Matt made them lose a half a day of blocking and taping and a half a day's worth of shooting, but Carsey-Werner never said, "Hey, you cost us this, Matt"—it was always "that bitch" cost us this and "that bitch" cost us that. He could've fixed it in a minute, and what writer wouldn't when the actress who's supposed to be the star of the show says she doesn't feel comfortable with a line?

Laurie Metcalf, the greatest actress in the world and a virtuoso human being, would tell me, "You know, they don't even see what you do, they don't even think it's acting. But anyone who can make Matt's lines funny is a *great actor.*" More than once I heard them complain: "Well, Roseanne is more of a stand-up than an actor." Well, stop giving me stand-up lines, give me something to do and I'll do it.

It got bad between me and Matt. Then it got worse.

When we'd rehearse, during blocking, the overhead microphones were on. *I didn't know that they had them on*, that they were able to monitor everything I said. One of the assistant directors on the show, Mark Samuels, came to me one day and discreetly walked me away from the set.

"I have to tell you," he whispered. "Those mikes are open. They leave them on, and they're listening to every word you say." It was a small thing, but I appreciated it, and to this day, Mark is still with the show.

So the lines were drawn, the sides were chosen (Matt had the size advantage, let me tell you), and the "Roseanne" set became the Gettysburg of ABC, the difference at Gettysburg being at least they fought humanely and had some ground rules. With the "Roseanne" show it was no holds barred. There were no DMZs, and that included my own body. Matt had this particularly despicable habit (tactic, really) of coming up behind me and touching me, prodding me in the back of the shoulder with his finger. To combat these stinky little digital incursions, I would have my sister, Geraldine, acting coach Roxanne Rogers, and my manager, Arlyne, stand around me in a circle to keep Matt away. Matt, being the horrid little terrier he is, would leap into the circle and lunge at me, just to touch me, just to exercise that power, the worst kind, which incorporates physical contact as a symbol for contamination, for colonization—a way of graphically showing you that you have no place to hide and that all of you was rendered onto Caesar. Jesus, it makes me puke to think of it, that an act that simple could be extruded into one of defilement, immolation, a sign of conquest. The 'art' of war.

After I learned that the mikes were live and I was being set upon by spies and tattletales, I took to doing a little warm-up exercise before the taping of the show. I turned the open mike into an electronic friend, and since a lot of people had trouble speaking to my face, I found a nice way to reach them.

"You cocksucker. I'm gonna fire your ass the first chance I get," I talked into the mike. "When my show—MY SHOW—reaches number one, your tweedy little ass is gonna be out on the fucking street. Write it down. Get the want ads out, you tumorous piece of shit, because you're history here." I'd continue the recital even as John Goodman, or whoever was in the upcoming scene, took their places on the set, and when the director hollered action—5, 4, 3, 2 . . . I became "Roseanne."

BORNE, STILL

was sixteen in 1968, when I got hit by a car, turned seventeen a few months later, and could never really catch up in school after that. Coming close to death *does* change a person. The accident was bad enough so that I had an out-of-body experience; my joke is I saw this lake of fire and heard everyone screaming. But the truth is, I awoke out of my coma changed, stranged, mangled, and fanged. I had no fear of death, no vulnerability, no memory.

That's why I saw a nuthouse in my immediate future. I fell behind in school after the car accident, and that year entered the laughing academy. To make matters special, I was on the floor with adults. Women. We left every day to go to school, down on the grounds. On the weekends I got to go home, which had to be unnerving for my parents, who had decided early on that all of the problems in my family had somehow to do with me. All roads led to Roseyville, a messy, chaotic town where, as parents, they were required to visit, but could never get out of quick enough or find a decent parking place. I was the designated patient.

I wanted so to get out of there. In the nuthouse, they put me on drugs and ran tests. I got out the following year, went home for three months, and promptly got pregnant.

I told my parents about the baby. That revelation led to me running away from home and moving into a real dumpy apartment on Second Street, south of Salt Lake City. The place was a bona fide fifty-dollar-a-month shithole, and to even afford that, I had to go on welfare.

I turned on the tap in the tub and roaches came out a little while before the orange water. When I went to the welfare office to get my welfare money, I saw kids there with the welfare eyes and smelled my own death. That's when I knew I couldn't keep my baby. No money to care for either of us properly. No support from my parents, who had no intention of letting me keep "an illegitimate kid." My dad spit on me. My dad *spit* on me.

I moved to a home for unwed mothers in Denver and my first child was adopted by a Jewish family there. The day after she was born I called my parents.

"Well, I had the baby," I said. My mother wanted to know what it was, a boy or a girl. Previously, she had made me promise never to tell her anything about my "bastard."

"You know, I don't really feel like telling you that," I said cautiously, caught off guard.

"Oh, please, I'm still the grandmother. Tell me."

"It's a girl."

"Is she cute?"

Yeah. As a matter of fact, she was beautiful. She had red hair. And one of her ears was bigger than the other, just like my mother. I felt like God gave that to her, a mark so I'd be able to find and identify her later. I got to hold her for a couple of days, knowing that in five days they were coming to get her. On the fifth day, my social worker came and said she was going to take me out to lunch—and I knew. I knew when we went out to lunch that they were going to take her. So before I went out, I embraced her, and whispered to her, "Have a nice life, Elisia," my name for her, "I'll see you in eighteen years." I kissed her good-bye and went out to lunch. After I lost my first child, my mother called me up:

"Me and your dad want to get in the car and come get you, bring you and the baby home."

"They already came and took the baby."

"Ohhhhhh, they did?" My mother moaned, as if she and Daddy had presented coupons for half-off at KFC and someone pointed out that they had expired a month earlier. "I didn't know that," she lied, saving face only to herself, I guess.

"Yes, you did. You definitely did. You know that they took my baby from me." Then I just hung up on her.

When I went home about five days later, my mom bound my breasts with these sheets because my milk was coming in. Then she told me she wanted to go out for a little ride to have a girl talk. Two blocks from the house, she asked:

"Roseanne, do you ever think about her?"

"You listen to me," I stammered, stunned. "I never want you to mention my baby or anything about her to me *ever* again. This fake concern you've got is sadistic. And when I find her I'm telling you right now you'll never see her. You're so fucking sick to ask me that. Don't ask me one more thing and you're never ever to talk to me about her." She knew I wanted to keep my baby but she never once offered her assistance, help, or concern. Her claims and cries—"What will the neighbors say?"—meant more to her than her own grandchild or daughter. And the neighbors were largely losers and insane or drunks.

I met my daughter again two days before her eighteenth birthday—exactly as I always knew I would because God promised me that. Two years later, after

Brandi (Elisia's new name was Brandi) and I had been re-
united, my mother got her phone number from a friend
of a friend (Jewish communities being very small out
west). She called Brandi's place and left a message on her
answering machine:

"Brandi, I want you to know that we don't hate
you." My mother has always said more in the spaces between the words than with the words themselves. . . .

I met Brandi face to face in L.A. I was walking into the
coffee shop of the Westwood Marquis Hotel. I was with
Geraldine and we were going to have a cup of coffee before going upstairs to meet Brandi and her mother, Gail.
My sister said, "My God, there they are!"

I looked over at a table in the corner and locked eyes
with my daughter for the first time in eighteen years. She
jumped up, I flew, we were entangled and locked together
like a powerful, unbreaking magnet. My sister pushed us
out of the coffee shop and into an elevator, saying "Go,
go!" as we were trying very hard to elude the tabloid media. All the way up in the elevator we clung. "I have
missed you so much," I cried and heard my brain commanding me: Breathe, walk, breathe, walk.

Our hands and feet and legs are the exact same. She
sings beautifully. Her voice reminds me of my grandmother's, who sang opera in Europe. Her sense of humor
matches my other children's. She was raised by loving
people, and I thank them.

Oh red-haired daughter
  from another life—

Our body brought you forth
    knowing you belonged to
    God only

Our arms held you for five days
      before you were
          taken
      from us, separated
          by war

Lost
You whispered as you were pulled
from me in your tiny blankets—

        Only eighteen years, Mother,
          I will see you soon.
When we talked inside the wind for all
          that time—
      in quiet gasps and wails of silenced
          music
Your little face was still recognizable to me
          caught in every
little child's face—

        I named you
        because God said to Elisia,
          "I will never leave you"
Wherefore eighteen years passed you came home
To me, across a universe, a sea and
an eon—and yet you are the same as the day
        We first held you
        and as tender

Back home after having my baby, from then on in, as an unwed mother in Utah, I was damaged goods. A friend of mine encouraged me to leave, telling me she had a place for me to go, knew some people in Georgetown, Colorado. I met Bill the night I arrived. He was literally the first guy I saw after I left my parents' home.

Bill, who, as a jackpot of admirable attributes, had a drinking problem. I was nineteen. I moved in with him two days later. Bill was from Colorado Springs, where they passed the antigay resolutions. His parents were typically right-wing, indigenous to that area at the time. Bill did a year of college, then moved on his own to L.A. to be a Sunset Strip hippie. Finding the work too demanding, he returned to Colorado and took a job as a night clerk in a motel.

It was total Norman Bates atmosphere, the toasted cheese sandwiches notwithstanding. He wouldn't let me sleep in the bed with him because he thought the owners might find us, so I slept in the closet on the floor, on some blankets. . . . Oh, well, he's protecting me—that's what I thought, extruded in my way of cutting the entire world some slack.

In the morning, I'd climb out of the window and come around to the front of the motel and, honing my acting skills even then, ask, "Is Bill here?"

Eventually, we became home owners, after a fashion. He bought a trailer—it was an eight-foot-wide job, about thirty feet long—small but certainly beyond the puny limits of his conception of domestic bliss. I redecorated the trailer with all this great contact paper. Then I got really assertive and I said to him,

"You know, if you die, none of this will be mine. And you have to marry me."

He goes, "Well, I figured I'd get married to you sooner or later."

"How 'bout sooner?" It was Albert Speer who once said some of the most profound decisions a man can make are made on a whim. Echt Bill. "Wellll . . . okay . . ." He shrugged. Then he didn't want a wedding unless it was in a cemetery, the cemetery across the street from our trailer. That is, if I wanted a so-called big wedding. I decided on a civil ceremony at city hall with just the two of us and no graves to avoid stepping on—except maybe our own. My parents, hoping to get us off on the right foot, sent me a check for twenty-five dollars (which helped, since I was making about twice that a week, working ten hours a day as a dishwasher), my grandmother sent a used toaster. By the way, for our honeymoon, we went to his friend's house and he got drunk while I sat on the bed and watched.

Within three months I was pregnant. I was happy as a dead hog smiling in the sun, having children that I was allowed to keep.

So I had no place to go, no skills, having dropped out of high school in the ninth grade after my accident.

Then, with the wave of a wand, so to speak, I had three kids. I stuck with Bill the postman for sixteen years, not so much out of habit, or masochism, but more out of survival. Hanging from a branch sticking out of an eroding cliff can be a real drag until you think of the alternatives. That branch suddenly looks like Prince Charming's arm.

In fact, at first, I was infatuated with Bill. When shopping for a man, I didn't bother checking the sticker for fancy options, I just took what was on the lot at the time. Gimme that stiff, sneering vinyl interior, and away we go. Gimme mean. Gimme shelter.

I'd spend entire days with Bill where he wouldn't talk to me—he'd just ignore me. When it came to chit-chat, he made Silas Marner look like Arsenio Hall. We just never spoke. At night, we'd go to bed and do it. That was the extent of our lovely relationship, a real quest for fire of grunts and emotional hoarding. I thought at first that Bill was just very shy, which made him even more charming for a short while, but the truth of it is he's just a weenie.

"I live in dire fear of having . . ." Bill trailed off one night, too mortified to continue.

"Of what? Come on, you can tell me." We were what you would call connecting in the Rockies.

"No. I can't talk about it. It's too horrible." I understood the not being able to talk part. That was a given with Bill. But the too horrible business was profoundly moving to me. Was he homicidal? Did he fear one day he'd take a man's life? His own life? Or was this another type of end? Was he afraid of turning gay?

"Of . . . of . . . having a bad acid flashback." And that's why he had to drink. Because that would put him to sleep at night.

Bill, to his credit, supported us all until I started doing stand-up. To his discredit, he didn't want me to work and he wouldn't let me have a car, either. He wanted me in the house, barefoot and pregnant, which worked out fine, for at the time I was suffering from agoraphobia. I didn't leave the house for two years.

I loved Bill though—no, I needed him because he was a big drunk and I needed to take care of somebody, so it was a totally codependent relationship, although I didn't know it at the time. After twelve tall-boy cans and a quart of beer a night, Bill would find a spot to lie in state in.

My man, I love him so, he'll never know. I wanted to be a good wife, raise a family, have a Hamburger Helper and Jell-O dinner waiting for my magnificent husband.

I wanted to, with all my heart, until Bill cheated on me while I was pregnant with my third kid in four years. After that, I could never trust or feel close to him again.

There was no great subterfuge, no Byzantine plots to conceal a torrid affair with some ski bunny or bar maid, or even some mysterious mail sorter with fast hands—no ladies' underwear in the glove compartment, no lipstick on the collar (Bill liked T-shirts), no contraband love letters in some stultifying backhand with big circles or little hearts to dot the *i*'s to let me know my marriage was in trouble—just Bill, who came home drunk, sat on the toilet with his pants around his ankles, and told me.

"Where have you been for the last eight hours?" I asked him. I was nine months pregnant and mincing words was never my long suit.

"Well," he said, looking straight at me, with a bit of arrogance, some male ego, and a little proud defiance, knowing he'd been drunk before, but never late: "I've been with a woman."

"I have a confession to make," he said to me in an assertive voice. "This happened to me because I'm ashamed of you because you're so fat. There. I finally said it," he confessed.

I took the kids and went to Motel 6. I sat there all night, came up with a dozen bowel-warming schemes, and, when none of them flew, went home in the morning to Bill, who'd slept enough to graduate his skin tone from stone-washed green to some vitamin-deficient shade of pewter.

I told him I wasn't gonna leave him, but as soon as I had the baby, I'd lose a ton of weight, and then get even. It was a plan hatched out of hate and misery, a plan that cost twelve dollars at Motel 6. I should write a country song about it. (After I had my son, I lost 120 pounds.

I decided to extract carnal revenge, and did. On top of that, I demanded to be allowed to have a part-time job selling women's clothing at a mall in Denver, as well as a driver's license and my own car, a lovely '62 Pontiac with rusted sides that was all mine for $200.)

The next day, Bill brought home a chair for me that fit snug and perfect under my sewing machine, as a "sorry" present and proof of his "luv."

LIVING ON MOUNTAIN TIME

was always funny. At nineteen, I worked at this restaurant in Georgetown, Colorado, washing dishes for fifty-six dollars a week and people would come in all the time just to see me. I'd wear this baseball suit that said LOVELAND REDI-MIX. My boss really liked me—in fact, most guys liked me, except for my husband.

As for Bill, he thought he was the most hilarious being ever to slink across the face of the earth. We'd go over to his friends' houses, he'd be sitting there, making jokes, making funny, until I'd chime in with something (usually a slam on him and his friends because together, they were about as funny as two little boys telling little-boy poop jokes). But whatever I said, they'd never laugh. It went on like that for years. He'd never laugh at my jokes. Number one, he was drunk. Number two, I was a woman, meaning my relationship with humor should have been as an object, not a perpetrator.

Once, after getting the same treatment—hey, I was cracking even *me* up, bringing down the house inside, but with Bill and his buddy, it was like telling jokes to a couple of deaf Mormons—I finally said something about it:

"You know, I never realized how deep sexism ran."

"Why, because we don't laugh at your little jokes?" Bill, not only the funniest man on the planet but in the festival of his own mind (much of which was closed down for seasonal repairs), the most clever as well, snorted back. I turned to him and I looked defiantly into his eyes, which I had never ever done before and I said: "Yeah. Yeah, that's right. Because my jokes are way funnier than yours." That was one of the first times I ever really spoke up to him. He was crushed for a week. I was the perfect wife until that day, modeling myself after his mother—the same woman who insisted that FDR was a communist and that women should have never been allowed to vote. Everything was the woman's fault, according to Bill and his mother. She was Phyllis Schlafly without the humor and the nice clothes.

Let's be honest. I was not always nice to Bill. To fall

back on the excuse that my husband just failed to bring out the best in me would be unfair (however true). There were many people, places, and things I hated and could not stomach but I managed to stay away from them rather than bring them into my home, have children with them, and put up with their toenail clippings. So, yeah, I made my own bed and, gulp, I had to sleep in it. But I also had to make Bill's life lousy now and then just to see if he could get more miserable, more flaccid, more vapor-locked in his own inertia, more stewed by his discontent, and I gotta say that sometimes was a real challenge.

After growing up in my family though, life with Bill and even life with his mother was a fairy tale. There was a modicum of security and kindness that now seems bleak but then was like being delivered to the promised land. Being a wife and mother and having a family were the most important and wonderful things I could've ever asked for. I was happy to have some logic, sense, and calmness in place of chaos and attack, which was all I had ever known before.

We used to frequent this drive-up hamburger joint that had this great big statue of a cowboy with a mechanical lasso that moved, back and forth. Right under him, off to the side, was a plywood cutout with his dialogue, and it said, "Howdy, pard!" We were sitting there eating when I kinda got silly and said, "Howdy, pard!" in this happy chipmunk voice. Bill chuckled a little, then actually laughed when I said it again, dragging it out,

"Howwwwwdy, parrrrd," then said it really fast, like a sped-up record. I kept saying it and Bill kept laughing but after about a half an hour, he just snapped.

"Don't say it anymore." He shook his finger at me in the car.

"Ohhhh, okay . . . *Howdy, pard.*" I snuck it in at the very end. Bill got out of the car in a big huff and smoked a cigarette, refusing to get back in until I promised I wouldn't say "Howdy, pard" again. He stayed out there for about six minutes until he solemnly opened the door and slid behind the wheel, all business. Don't do it, don't do it, don't do it, I chanted to myself, don't do it, don't do it. "Howdy, pard," I said in an almost inaudible murmur. Bill, hunched over the wheel, glared at the road, and he screamed with such force that there was spit all over the dashboard because I kept saying "Howdy, pard" over and over like I had Tourette's syndrome (which I found out later is really called OCD and I'm on Prozac for it), until I finally let it go.

About six months later, I was on my way into the kitchen when Bill caught my eye. He was stretched out on the couch, making a little fort around himself with tall-boy beer cans, and he had a sleepy, maudlin smile on his face, as though at that moment he was taking a wobbly stab at this notion that we were a team, man and wife, *confidants*, me and him against the world. That, or he was just plain horny. He held me captive with his dumbstruck stare and drew me to the couch, the blush of ardor high in my cheeks matching the crimson of his eyes. I bent over the torn back of the couch and whispered, "Howdy, pard." Three years after our divorce, when we hated each other, I called Bill and said it over the phone. This time he laughed.

I added "Howdy, pard" to my bag of surgeon's tools that I used, throughout the wavering course of our marriage, to dissect routinely his peace of mind and perform angioplasty on the fatty arteries of his smugness.

I got some relief from Bill working at Gigi's dress shop as a window dresser. Then I heard about a restaurant called Bennigan's. The guy who ran the place was so impressed with how outgoing and big-breasted I was that he created a whole job for me. I got to be cocktail waitress at the bar, and had my own hours—just four hours a night, but the tips were awesome and I was pretty good, if I don't say so myself. Also it helped that I didn't have to serve food because I was a horrible waitress. I used to come out of there with 50 percent tips—partly because I never gave anyone their change—but also because I was funny.

"How much for the drinks?" a customer would ask. I always charged twice as much as they were supposed to be and usually got away with it. People are just not assertive enough to make a stink over paying a ten-dollar bill for a six-dollar check and not getting change. It was pretty awful of me and I actually got caught twice, once for shortchanging guys who gave me fif-

ties. I claimed they were twenties. Another time a woman caught me:

"I was at that table the last time you pulled this
stunt," she hissed. "Now I want my goddamn change or
I'm gonna get your ass fired."

Around the time I started working at Gigi's, I got a
call from my sister, Stephanie, who was living with my
parents in Utah. She was whispering. Big pauses, maybe
a minute between every word.

"What, what?" I prodded her.

"Well, I'm in my room and I haven't left my room
for two weeks."

"Come on, what's a matter?"

"Well, something happened." So what in the fuck is
going on? You know, I panicked, thought she was going
to tell me somebody was dead or something. She tells me
Daddy did something.

"Well, what did he do? Did he beat the fuck out of
you or what?"

"No, he"—big, big pause, still whispering—"put his
hand down my pants." She was seventeen, an A student,
and had won the Hope of America award—which meant
she was nothing like me, which also meant, in some sorry
mutation of ideal parenting, that my father didn't play favorites. Stephanie later denied that Daddy abused her, but
at that moment, she was looking for help. I told
Stephanie to get the hell out of there. Don't sit there one
more second. Take money from her Bat Mitzvah fund,

cash it in, and buy a plane ticket to Denver now. Don't bring any clothes. Just get on the plane and get out of there. And she did. She was there the next day. When she showed up I asked her what she told Mom and Dad.

"Well, I told them I was coming to see you, you know, like I do all the time." Only this time it was different. The two of us sat in the kitchen going over and over things, not only trying to sort out what was real, but how to define it, both of us—all of us—suffering from a kind of emotional dyslexia. Children have a way of idealizing their parents, of spinning gold where there was/is straw. Daddy was hard, crusty shale, formed from molten hillbilly. He was all wind and piss—but none of us wanted to believe he was a child abuser. But ours was a truth based on the same kind of denial that has you believing for most of your life that you'll never die. When Steph talked, it was horrible, so horrible, in fact, that it seems odd to me now that the whole affair didn't trigger my own memories. In a small, elliptical way, it actually did; I remember saying, "Well, Daddy didn't do anything different than he always did—right?" Since being molested and touched inappropriately was a regular part of our lives, it seemed rather normal, as my memories rose and flared, my belly leaped and receded. But something was there. I called my mother and told her what Steph had said.

"Well, that's totally ridiculous," she denied, and in the next breath, gave him an out. "If he did do anything, it's because he's on heart medication and he didn't mean anything by it. She's just trying to cause trouble. You don't believe her, do you?"

"Well, yeah. She's pretty shook up, yeah, I do. Something happened."

"Maybe he grabbed her or something when he was on the drug and she took it wrong. You know how she gets overly dramatic about everything."

"You got to talk to her about it at least," I told her. "She's got to get this straightened out. She's all ripped up. You have to do something."

"Well, I'm not going to tell your dad because it will kill him. He just had a bypass and this will kill him." When I finally got Mom to agree to talk to her, Steph got off the phone, crying. Mom accused her of making the whole thing up. Right. That's why she wouldn't eat, wouldn't dress, wouldn't come up out of the basement. That's why she weighed about eighty-five pounds, why she had anorexia since she was eight. She had the youngest case of it anyone ever heard of. Nobody even knew what it was. They just called it the starving disease. And the real reason why most people commonly get it is because it's from sexual trauma, like overeating is. My parents said that they were told the reason she had it was because a lot of girls who have an older sister who's fat get it. Boy, my fat gives everybody an out. There has to be a lot of shit going on in a family for a girl to want to retard her body so it doesn't get curves or any sexuality.

Or for a girl to make her body so big that it has no sexuality. That's what eating disorders are really about.

I didn't call my mother for a while after that 'cause I was just lost. Steph talked to her a few weeks later.

"Well, Mom believes me," she said. I called Mom and asked her about it.

"I told her I *believe* that something is bothering her. I didn't tell her I believed what she *said*," Mom corrected. And then I said, "You know, this is going to tear your whole family apart and we're not going to be able to have relationships or see each other if you don't talk about this." She had the solution the next time I heard from her. Her master plan was to have me take custody of Steph, and to make it all kosher, my mother had this paper drawn up and had it notarized, this piece of paper that said I was Steph's legal guardian. Which was all the same to me. I was used to it.

I was eleven years old when she was born. Mom was working in other people's homes as a domestic all day and taking care of other people's kids. By the time I was twelve, I went to school, then came home, cleaned the house, and cooked dinner almost every day. If my dad came home and the house wasn't clean, he went into a frenzy. Everything was up to me. I was the substitute mom.

About two months later, my other sister, Geraldine, moved from Utah to Denver to join us. She had been living with this married woman who had two children. The woman's Mormon husband had a private detective follow them and was going to use her lesbianism against her in court to try and take her kids away. So she asked Geraldine to move out. Geraldine also knew Steph was living with me so she figured, I'll go to Denver, too.

Geraldine, who made a habit out of moving in with women and allowing them to support her in return for her "brilliant" Maimonidean commentaries on sex, religion, pop psychology, and post–Bat Mitzvahn Zionist history and ethics.

Geraldine, who worked as my assistant in L.A., had a full "beard" then, which I at first suggested she tint, then dye, then electrocute. She refused for political reasons. She would not "sell out to the Hollywood fuckers, those woman-hating bastards" that stood in the way of herself and millions of dollars intended for her and her lover, Maxine. Together, they would one day return to Jerusalem and Paris in order to spread the word and cause of Lesbian Feminist Separatism to Israeli, Palestinian, and Parisian women in the cause of anti-Patriarchal world peace.

She would continually recount with shock and anger how she had talked to a specific person (on my behalf, mind you) and all they had done was stare at her face.

"Well then, if you aren't going to shave it, then don't use it to fire up your anger all the time. Groom it, shape it, and BE PROUD!" I offered.

"Oh, Rose," she laughed, "we're such Utah geeks."

"Yes, but that is what these geeks out here will call 'refreshing.' You don't need the beard, sis. You are a true Utah geek. That bleeds through all of our Barr family lineage. You can safely shave and still be a freak of nature." Oh, what a laugh we had over that one. She used Jolen bleach on it for about two months and then, unable to withstand any form of "female mutilation," she let it grow black again.

In Denver, then, that was our new family: three sisters, my husband, Bill, and the kids. First thing we did was get Steph a cheap counselor at a mental health center and then enroll her in high school. At night, all the sisters would sit around the kitchen table trying to figure out our lives. We had to figure out why males control. We had to figure out Patriarchy. We had to devise a plan to Get Males. Every day we'd do hours and hours of male control, Patriarchy, men are rapists and pigs. This was so much more comfortable than saying our father molested us.

Well, you become an expert when you're ignorant or in denial. That's what we did. We were experts on women's issues. Geraldine brought the feminist/lesbian perspective to the table. I was always a feminist, or at least angry. Meanwhile, my husband sat there drinking his ass off every day. He'd relate to my sisters by telling them while I was at work that I was going really, really crazy. Bill, the cock of the walk, didn't care for Geraldine, but he liked Steph because she was younger. And in Steph, he finally found someone who would pay attention to his UFO theories and beliefs of space aliens visiting Earth and readying to return. She, in turn, found a new big brother, that is, until he started talking to her about our married life and then she'd become horribly uncomfortable. He used her as a sounding board for his complaints about me, i.e., he told her that I never took a bath anymore. This was true. And not only had I stopped bathing, I started saying I was going to become a writer. A really famous writer.

My mother would put in an occasional goodwill call, just to see how the sisters were faring. She'd drag Daddy to the phone, make him get on.

"All right, this is costing money, hello, good-bye, how are you? I'm fine, you're fine, bye." That was the sum total of his conversation every time. I'm fine, you're fine, costing money, hello, good-bye. That's one of the things we thought was so humorous and charming about him—before we started therapy.

After about a year, Stephanie decided that she was going to go back to Salt Lake. Moved back in with my parents, then proceeded to make their lives miserable. Just the usual passive/aggressive teen stuff, like go out drinking, stay out all night, etc. She met this boy who was a male prostitute, actually quite famous in Utah at the time, responsible for bringing down a senator or congressman or such, who frequented boy prostitutes and was caught. She moved in with the boy just to torment my parents, feeling it to be her only option. By the time she went back home to Salt Lake she had it totally twisted in her head that the whole incest episode was irrelevant, and her real problem was that I made her quit high school and move to Denver. She had transferred everything angry that belonged to my parents to me. I remember this therapist I once had who said people hate their rescuer. If you're not going to deal with your abuse or look at your life and work out your problems, you might as well blame someone for them. I thought at the time that this was one of the most painful things I'd ever have to deal with. I was wrong.

Things got dangerously out of hand, working at Bennigan's. On my break I would go out to my customers' cars with them—needless to say, I was on a sexual acting-out binge. As soon as I got to cocktail city, it was wham-bam, thank you, ma'am. Worst of all, I was charging for it. Most of the time I couldn't remember how many sets of bleary eyes I tried looking into for some sign of life outside of a blood-engorged organ. I could feel myself slipping away, into the foam of the sea, pulling away like loose rock, falling deeper and deeper into a well that started in the back of my head. I stopped sleeping almost totally at this time, yet I was hardly ever tired. Sex became the most horrifying and disgusting thing in the world to me, and I could not bear for my husband to touch me. Yet I would find myself in cars with strange men often, in partial or full nudity, something else foreign to my conscious mind: It had taken seven years for me to be naked in front of Bill. The thought of it horrified me.

I would "wake up" when the money was handed to me and think, "Am I being a whore, now?" Memories would drift in and out, foggily, of times in tenth grade when I would find myself walking across town at three in the morning, barefoot and nearly naked.

One of these times I was picked up in the afternoon by truant officers and brought to school, then taken home to Mommy. She threatened to have me locked up and it was not long after that that she did. I had lost it then, at age seventeen, and now at twenty-seven, I was losing it again, completely.

I would forget what I was doing almost immediately after doing it. I would bring my money home and buy groceries and toys with it. Now it seems it was the only way I had of pushing down vague fears and memories of sexual darkness from a young, young faraway time.

The sex was one thing. But I used to eat off of people's plates, too. Yeah. Chow down on a stranger's leftovers and then go vomit. I got trench mouth from that; well, I don't really know if I got it from eating people's nachos or having sex with them, but I do know that they promptly laid me off at the lounge when my teeth kept bleeding.

After I was orally presentable again, they allowed

me back. I had a little cadre of fans who either got my humor or were just happy I hadn't stiffed them. One guy told me how funny I was. They would say, you know you oughta go down to the Comedy Shoppe and do an act. I call this moment my awakening because ever since I was three, I knew I was gonna be a comedian. I suppose all the time in between I was just waiting. I didn't know how, but I knew it was gonna happen.

It took me six months to write a five-minute act (see my first book). I'd get an idea, like, say, my husband wants me to be more aggressive in bed. Then I'd just write about it in my notebook, pages and pages, just to get one joke, kind of the way it takes a whole bunch of tree sap to make a bottle of syrup. Only my jokes are a little less sweet. You set up the premise, the hook, then the punchline. But that's just the beginning. You can be a real witty bastard in writing and people will chuckle. But stand-up happens at the speed of light. The material has to work in the delivery.

That first act was purely political, really nasty, pro-woman, filled with everything that you're never ever supposed to say. I tried it out on Bill and he approved. The funniest thing about it, though, was that he never knew whom I was talking about and neither did I, really—but it was always him. Him and my Daddy. It got to be that everything he did, I put in my act. In this way, Bill made me a scientist the way Jerry Lewis was in *The Nutty Professor*. I observed, extrapolated, had an alter-existence, then blew up the results all over the place, with spotlights as my Bunsen burner. Bill always thought I was talking about lesser-evolved males than himself. That, however, was not possible, since my act was not about amoebas.

"Can you believe that asshole said that?" Bill would always act astonished when he'd hear a particularly nasty racist or sexist joke. Then he'd turn around and repeat it to his friends like it was his own. For a while, I thought he was just doing a great parody on racist and sexist attitudes, until later I realized it was no parody. Now that I think of it, I had a habit of indulging Bill the way you would a retarded child. When I first met Tom on the comedy circuit, I told him about Bill.

"He's such a great poet," I remember gushing. "You may not see it, but he is a great poet, a great parodist. Now when Bill sues me, which is regularly, Tom always shrugs: "Well, he's a poet, honey. A great poet."

At this time I was (a) working in a feminist bookstore, (b) doing stand-up comedy, (c) walking the streets or picking up audience members to fleece for sex and money, (d) going home to be a full-time housewife and mother, (e) writing for a lesbian/feminist publication called *Big Mama Rag* in Denver, (f/g) conducting two full-time affairs, and (h) trying to write for *Heavy Metal* magazine. Busy, busy, busy. Luckily, "I" was somehow able to do them all, with various levels of success.

My comedy career took off out of the bookstore I helped run, chasing out MALES with a big baseball bat before changing in my car and walking four blocks down the street to hustle them.

I started telling my jokes in the parking lot of the bookstore to about fifteen to thirty-five politically active lesbians who encouraged, laughed at, and supported me by coming to my shows, especially the ones I did at the local comedy club, where shocked patrons would stare mutely at me while I did my "act." They would roar loudly, until the regular crowd finally understood that I was funny, not castrating, since the joke was not on ME, something unheard of for a woman comic at the time, 1980.

These women would allow me to perform at their coffeehouses and talent shows and laugh loudly at the same shit they had heard three hundred times before. They made me popular in Denver, they made it safe for me there, too, in comedy. Now you know why I try accurately and respectfully to have lesbians portrayed on all my shows. Thanks, gals, here's to ya! Thankfully, there was only ever one big fat dyke who told me I would be allowed to perform only if I changed all my jokes to be about sex with women instead of men. Hello? Hello?

ZIT-GEIST
AND SACRED
BULLS

"*H*ey—*I have real American breasts. That's right. You know why? Because they're red, white, and blue. Red stretch marks, big blue veins, and the whitest skin you'll ever see this side of Cherry Hills village. Christ, haven't you ever seen a National Geographic?"*

(Not enough laughs. Okay, try this one on for size, you peckerwoods.)

"I tried this new feminine deodorant spray that was invented by a woman gynecologist, guaranteed to drive

men wild, make them fight to the death to get next to you because it smells just like money."

I started headlining comedy clubs about eight months after I started, which is pretty incredible, especially for a woman, because they weren't into booking any women headliners in the clubs at that time. I was a giant curiosity, something people had to see, like an apartment fire or some prehistoric creature that had found its way into a tidal pool. Part of it was I was the filthiest act ever. People couldn't believe the stuff I would do, and I would do anything.

Once I went on stage, that was the last day I was gonna kiss any ass. I had that great feeling that I was *all there*, totally present. It made up for how wretched my life had been until then. Because the number one rule for stand-up is that you gotta be a real pitiful, yet hateful bastard. I couldn't wait to get up there and kick some ass. 'Cause I took too much shit my whole life. Which is not to say people stopped taking bites outa my ass after I became a comic. I took all kinds of heat for my act.

Ed Nichols, the owner of the Comedy Works, was one of many who read me the riot act. You can't say this, you can't say that. On and on and on.

"Half the audience already hates you," Ed complained.

"Yeah, which half?"

"The men, that's who." He was wrong, of course.

Men loved me. "And the women, if their husbands are uncomfortable, they're not gonna laugh. And another thing. I'm not booking you back in this club unless you drop that Kennedy joke." Part of my act was about the difference between male comics and female comics. "For instance, Lenny Bruce said Jackie Kennedy was climbing out of the limo in Dallas to save her own ass. That's Lenny, the archetypal male comic. See, that's the male perspective. I'm a woman and I know that was never, never true. She wasn't climbing out to save her own ass. She sees her husband's brains sliding down the back of the car. She's going out there because she's trying to clean up the mess!" I used to get standing ovations in some clubs for telling that joke, always in the jazz clubs. I like to bring down the sacred cows.

Eventually, I was banned from the comedy clubs in Denver altogether. Unitarian churches, dyke bars, punk clubs would still have me; these were the hostels where I could spread the word without having it snatched from me or kneaded into some kind of tasteless/tasteful fritter for popular consumption. But my best gig was as an emcee of a strip show. My partner was another woman comic named Susan. We were paid fifty bucks a night each, which was unheard of back then. We got more and more outrageous at the strip club and I was acting-out horribly by then. I had no fear.

"We'd like to do our impressions of the strippers for all of you," Susan and I announced to a packed audience one night. The whole place started hooting, hollering—they thought we were gonna take our clothes off. Instead, we started kissing each other.

"These strippers are lesbians," I shouted between kisses. "They hate you. Have you ever thought of that? You're all just johns, assholes with money, do you know that?"

"YOU CAN'T DO THAT IN FRONT OF A MALE AUDIENCE," everyone shouted at me. "They'll turn on you. THEY'LL HATE YOU." People stood in line to read me the riot act, from club owners, to Bill, to my sisters. Here's what I figure reading the riot act really means: Shut up and do what you're told. It never means nothin' more than that. All my life people have read me the riot act. They all read me the riot act and I suppose since, early on, I developed the uncanny ability to be visible and yet not present, I'd forget about it all in two minutes anyway. I kept coming back. If I did not know how to dissociate, I'd be crazy today.

So while people who supposedly knew better shook their fingers at me, I kept doing my rude, sloppy, lampoon-the-male act. The thing was, once they started laughing, they loved it. Surprisingly, men loved my act—as raunchy as it was—I expected it to be threatening and overpowering as prophesied but they liked it. They loved jokes about how stupid they were. They loved it not so much because it was the truth (I don't have the bar graphs and the stat sheets to prove it, just take my word for it) but because, as Santayana once said, the only true dignity of man is his capacity to despise himself. Or maybe it's all that dominatrix-whore shit they got going, I don't know. Maybe I just tapped into some weird guy–type Zit-geist.

It was at this time as well that I went the Virginia Woolf route, taking on a lover. He had a shaved head and was a bisexual intravenous drug user. I always did pick the classiest guys. But he did plays about Dylan Thomas in a theater that he started. On the weekends, he'd have jazz groups and he'd let me come on and do my act with the jazz guys and that was awesome. It was his idea so I guess I owe him a debt of thanks, although I have no idea where he is today. I heard that after we broke up, he joined a kibbutz in Israel. But he let me work with these jazz bands and it did something to my consciousness as a comedian. The rhythms got in my brain and shook loose the convention, like dirt off of a radish root—it got me into the music of talk.

YOU'LL GET AIRLINE JOKES, HAIRLINE JOKES,
AND THE ALL-TIME FAVORITE, "TAKE MY WIFE,
PLEASE."
BUT, SERIOUSLY, FOLKS,
YOU'LL GET ALL THE JOKES BOYS LOVE TO TELL!
THAT'S RIGHT, FRIENDS!
PENIS JOKES FOR EVERY OCCASION,
THE LONG AND THE SHORT OF IT.

BUT YOU WON'T GET THE SHAFT,
'CAUSE THERE'S A MONEY-BACK GUARANTEE IF
YOU'RE NOT SATISFIED.

YES! GRAB 'EM, PULL 'EM, AND HOLD ON TO
THEM, BOYS!
EXPRESS ALL THE WONDER AND GLORY THAT IS
YOURS AS A MALE!
(WHY DO YOU THINK THEY CALL IT STAND-UP,
KID?)

AND SAY, I LOVE DRUGS, YOU LOVE DRUGS,
EVERYBODY WE'VE EVER KNOWN IN OUR LIVES
LOVES DRUGS.
AND NOW, ON ONE COMEDY RECORDING
YOU GET ALL THE GREAT DRUG JOKES OF THE
SIXTIES.
YES, OPIATES ARE THE RELIGION OF THE
MASSES.
AND THE FIRST ONE'S FREE, KID! HEY! HEY!
FEATURING THE JOKES OF A BYGONE ERA,
BEFORE WE ALL "JUST SAID NO!"

YOU GET ALL THE FUNNY LADIES.
YOU'LL GET MARTHA RAYE, DORIS DAY, ELAINE
MAY, MINNIE PEARL, AND MILTON BERLE!
YOU'LL GET BILL COSBY, NORM CROSBY, ALAN
KING, SHECKY GREENE, DON RICKLES, AND
MIKE NICHOLS!
YOU'LL GET MARTY ALLEN, FRED ALLEN,
GRACIE ALLEN, WOODY ALLEN, AND STEVE
ALLEN . . . THE FUNNIEST GENTILE OF THEM
ALL!

YOU'LL GET THE GREAT COMEDY TEAMS; W. C.
AND TOTIE FIELDS, SHARI AND JERRY LEWIS,
AND THE FAMOUS MARX BROTHERS . . .
GROUCHO AND KARL.
YOU'LL GET BENNY. WOW!
HENNY! . . . "A GUY WALKS INTO A
PSYCHIATRIST'S OFFICE . . ."
AND LENNY . . . "WHAT THE FUCK ARE WE
DOING IN VIETNAM, MAN?"

THAT'S RIGHT.
LENNY BRUCE RECORDED LIVE AT HIS LAST
PERFORMANCE, "LENNY,"
WITHOUT PUNCHLINES,
ABOUT A WEEK BEFORE HE SADDLED UP THE
FLOOR,
AND RODE IT INTO THE SUNSET.

I played in some pretty weird places.

When I first went on stage, I was really thin and I dressed provocatively—I think I slid through just from the men hooting at me, I dunno. It would probably take about five minutes each time to get them to stop hooting—I wore fishnet stockings and revealing tops, big heels. Then I went into my act, which was this real radical feminist thing. That was the point—to mix messages all the way—something I've always been fascinated with until I started therapy.

The Comedy Shop eventually banned me from the club for my material. To protest, I produced a woman's show, in Boulder, Colorado, called "Take Back the Mike." I had all the press come, as well as my thirty-five-lesbian-member fan club.

"If you're a woman with something to say, you're not allowed to say it on a stage in Denver—that's why I'm producing this show. THE COMEDY SHOPPE WILL NOT ALLOW ME TO *PERFORM*." Back at the Comedy Shoppe, they read the papers, got really scared, and invited me back. By the time I went back, my intellectual prostitute act had evolved with some major fits of inspiration into the housewife act. Prostitutes are just glorified housewives anyway, I used to say. No one ever got that but me and maybe some other ex-prostitute housewives.

MISTER
TOM ARNOLD

"You're really gonna like this guy who's opening for you," Scott Hanson, the owner of the
Comedy Club in Minneapolis was telling me,
as we were climbing the stairs.

"I hate male comics."

"Now, Roseanne. Be open-minded—"

"For what. So I can hear more smelly-pussy jokes
and sexist shit like that?"

"Now, Roseanne—"

"Here's me following some jerk male comic—'And

now we have a female comed-*ienne*'—and then bring me out after two hours of dick jokes."

"Well, you're gonna like this guy," Scott insisted. Yeah, yeah, yeah, whatever. I had learned the ways of the stand-up world by now anyway, and rule number one for headliners (which I was) was you always check out the new comic's act before you talk to him. It might be humiliating in the long run to say "Hello" to an idiot who wasn't funny. And any guy I'd ever worked with before was always horrifyingly threatened by me (beginning with Bill, and that wasn't even a professional partnership).

This guy comes up the stairs—he's late, as he still is to this day—his face as lit up as a full moon, eyes all eager and parrying, he's got this, this pull to him, like he's on a leash and he's trying to buck his owner, his feet making these crazy little nervous dance steps or something.

"Hi," Tom Arnold says, really nervous. You have to understand that I did have somewhat of a reputation by now as a female with a slight chip on her shoulder (let's be real—I was the Hunchback of Notre Dame), and it was rumored that I had a mean streak that could make a rattler stand up and run. Hey—the world makes you into a bitch, no matter how quietly you go, so you may as well go kicking and screaming. Get out of my way and save me the time.

"Listen," I ups and says to Tom, "you don't do any

pig-type shit, do ya?" I always said that to guys to get 'em shook up, cuz the headliner has the power to can the opening acts.

"What'd'you mean, like sexist stuff?"

"Yeah, because I really hate to follow that kind of slime."

"Oh, no, no. I don't do any kind of sexist stuff. Not at all," he trailed off, then added, "Well, I call women cum dumpsters and hosebags and stuff like that. Is that okay?" This baby-faced grin . . . And I completely cracked up. And I was ashamed of myself for cracking up 'cause not less than an hour ago I had been in my hotel room taking notes from a book on radical feminist theology. But it was just funny that somebody dared to do that because it was me, my reputation, preceding me.

"Hey, uh, so . . . you wanna do some coke or something?" Tom more wondered than asked, like if I said no, it sure as hell wasn't gonna stop him. I did a noseful of it. It was one of the first times for me. Tom got up to do his set and he was hard to follow. I stood there watching his act and I could not believe it—he was so funny. He did this whole disastrously botched magic act with live goldfish and broke every rule that you could think of. He killed the fish, set them on fire in front of the audience— really brilliantly horrible—and people loved it because it was just so absolutely vile, you just had to laugh. He had this undercurrent of uncomfortableness, an awkward hickdom propellant, but more like a guy who wants to behave but just can't seem to help himself, a guy who's learned to live with always being sorry for something.

Scott Hanson, for example, weighed about seven hundred pounds. He'd emcee, too, and after doing his routine, he'd pass Tom backstage.

"Don't do any fat jokes about me. My wife and my family are here tonight. Any other night but tonight, okay?"

"You got it, buddy," Tom assured him. Then Tom would go on and do twenty minutes' worth of fat jokes about Scott. He'd grab the stage curtain and holler, "Scott, you forgot your pants! Ladies and gentlemen, Scott's very sensitive about his weight. You know, I had a dream that Scott died . . . and the funeral looked like a tractor-pull. Christ, there's such a thing as overweight, and then there's having to piss in a bucket, okay?" Just so mean, and every night the guy would swear he wasn't gonna do it again. Then he'd go up and do the pants joke.

And I was in awe because I thought I was the only one who wasn't trying to be like Steve Martin or Jerry Seinfeld. I mean, we were both out there; we both knew what The Smallness of It All was, we saw it, hunted it down, found it and got scared shitless by it, but got some relief from the laughs—a life of one's own in exchange for a life of stand-up.

We became best buddies that first time we met and watched each other's act. Later he invited me to a party.

We went to this house that other comics lived in and we partied all night. Tom took me up to this room, which I thought was his room, till five years later, when he told me *he* really didn't live there. Tom, in fact, didn't live anywhere. He slept on people's couches. Up in this room that wasn't his, we slept side by side, huddled on top of a sleeping bag. There was nothing sexual at all between us. It was like meeting your doppelganger.

Tom started writing jokes for me after that, and on my tours, I took him as my middle act. Which was kind of an excuse just to hang out with him, 'cause I just loved seeing him. I'd go home and it was not very fun there, but every six weeks or so, when I had a gig, with Tom as my middle, I had a riot. I thought when we saw each other, we would just party real hard, drink, get high, and that would be it, but then I'd go home and I wouldn't do it again until I saw him. However, he kept it up all year long.

And we got more and more crazy on the road. Our biggest fun was to go to comedy clubs and heckle other comics. I used to go heckle Andrew Dice Clay all the time, in Los Angeles—I loved to heckle him the most. Some of those nasty lines he got are from saying that stuff to me: "Here's to you. Sucking my dick." We were good friends, too. Andrew is one of the nicest guys on the planet. And back then, Sam Kinison was really funny, too, and very instrumental in helping me come to Los Angeles. People would walk out in the middle of his show and he'd say, "Hey, where're you going? Home to the sexual disappointment that awaits you? Give me a list of your sacred dead. SO I CAN WIPE MY ASS ON IT!" He would do great Lenny Bruce–like routines, about Jesus, religion and hypocrisy. But he fell on hard times, too. Drugs killed him like they killed Lenny, Belushi, Freddy Prinze, dozens of others not so well known who came to, as Leonard Cohen says, "Say it clear, say it bold."

Jackie Diamond is a brilliant comic. His act is part pimp on Jerry Lewis, part pimp on the whole Catskills/ Borscht Belt realm. First time I saw him was at a club in San Francisco. He comes up on stage and takes a seat on a stool with two huge black bodyguards with sunglasses standing on either side of him. He starts singing this schlocky show tune, while the bodyguards act like they're scanning the audience for anybody who might rush the stage. Then Jackie starts his monologue with "I come from a little street called Tin Pan Alley . . . ," really patronizing and melancholy. Just terrific. I caught him again at the Comedy Store and he just killed. Sam, who was on before Jackie, just couldn't handle it if anyone was funnier than him. He walked right out on stage during Jackie's act and started giving him shit.

"Sam, get off the stage and give Jackie his time. You've already had your time," Harry Basil, another comedian, yelled from the audience. Harry, whose act involved playing music from TV shows and movies, never liked Sam to begin with, so I figured this was gonna be good.

"FUCK YOU, METAL HEAD!" Sam shouted down from the stage. "If somebody lost your fucking tapes, you wouldn't even have a fucking act! You can't even ad-lib, you dumb shit!" Just vicious Sam stuff. And that would make anybody shut up and slink away, but Harry was really drunk or something. He goes, "Oh, yeah—?" and he stood up on a table, pulled his pants down, and mooned Sam on stage. "I KNOW LORNE MICHAELS, I KNOW RODNEY DANGERFIELD, I KNOW BON JOVI— AAAAAHHHHHGGG!" Harry pimped Sam's trademark holler. Sam was in full-metal insult mode by now, railing away on stage, while Harry turned the whole crowd against him.

"Don't let him get away with this, the arrogant bastard," Harry beseeched the audience. "I want everyone in this room to get up and leave. Right now. Everyone follow me! I'll buy the pizza! I'll pay for your cab fare! I want you all to walk out on him because he's an arrogant, hateful, insecure motherfucker!" And damned if everybody—almost five hundred people—didn't get up and walk out. It was incredible! Sam comes down from the stage, sits next to me.

"*Can you believe that?*" He's searching my face for an answer.

"This was the best night of comedy I've ever seen!" I said back to him. We laughed.

I love Rodney Dangerfield. He's so unbelievably dark. And so sad. He'll get real intense, get right into your face. Outa his mind comes the truest, meanest things in the world. This is Rodney: We were walking down Ocean Boulevard in Santa Monica some time ago. He strolls right out in the middle of traffic, making cars stop, screech, slam on their breaks. I said, "Rodney, we're gonna get killed, we should wait for the light."

"Are you kiddin' me," he squawks over his shoulder, in that way of his that makes you think of neck problems. "We're not gonna get killed—I'm a draw."

As we're walking we see this poor black kid in a wheelchair, his whole body is all twisted. He looked like a thalidomide baby, a big old head and just these gnarled fingers. As we're walking past him the little boy calls out in a distorted voice, "Rodney Dangerfield—I want to shake your hand." So Rodney agrees and shakes his hand.

Rodney whispers to me as we're walking away. "Well, kid—you got no arms, no legs, and you're black. Got your whole life aheada ya, huh?" I fell over.

Rodney and I had the good fortune of turning up at this Pritikin Diet Center together. Rodney and I used to sneak out to smoke cigarettes and eat. I remember one of the first times we entered the dining room. Rodney looked around and said, "Boy, I tell ya—this is the wrong time of year to come here, look at all these Hebes. At least the goys, they show a little fear—a little respect.

They're afraid to walk too close to you because they don't want to offend you. The Jews come right up to you and say, 'Move over—I saw you in Vegas last month and you sucked.'"

I saw him a couple months ago, he said, "Heh, heh, Roseanne—you look good, what happened? What, are you wearing makeup?"

So Tom and I heckled other comics. And did a lot of drugs. What I didn't know was that Tom was doing even more than that. We went to Denny's one night and he got up from the table with a blowtorch in his hand—and he goes in the bathroom and smokes crack.

"You won't believe this guy," I said to Bill, slipping a videotape of Tom's act into the machine. And Bill loved him. When Tom and me were on the road, he'd talk to Bill and they became friendly. Tom had a fiancée—well, he had five of them in the years that I knew him—and like me, he tended to pick partners who hated him. There's plenty of codependents out there who can't wait to get into a relationship like Mom and Dad had. Anyway, I didn't think anything romantic would happen; I was already married forever to this Bill guy and would be for the rest of forever. I figured I'd probably cheat on him sometimes, whenever it got really, really lonely. Besides, Bill was funny, too. Not as funny as he thinks he is, but he was good for a joke now and then. He actually became a comic and worked in the same club as me. Bill did conceptual stuff, bits about old ladies in cafeterias who put their perfume on with a ladle, the fumes drifting into the kitchen and starting a fire—that kinda thing. And Bill saw Tom as "the buddy." The first time Tom told me, some years later, that he loved me, he said, "Well, what did you think? Did you think that it was gonna be, 'Hi, come on in. This is my husband, my kids, and my buddy?' " And I did think it was gonna be like that—my buddy, Tom, along with the husband, kids, and fiancée forever.

CHAPTER 6

A PERSONAL GUARANTEE FROM CARNAC

S
o I had this six-minute act that I'd been working on for five years. After headlining clubs on the road, my comic friends were telling Mitzi Shore about me and urging me to come to L.A. to perform at her place. Louie Anderson and Sam Kinison jacked up Mitzi for me. The first time I did the six minutes for Mitzi Shore and a crowd at her Comedy Store, I killed. They had never heard anything like what I was sayin'. Because at that time it was like, "Are women comics feminine?" That kind of stuff. Johnny Carson had just done

an interview with *Rolling Stone,* where he said women comics aren't funny because they lose their femininity. I broke every rule. I said: "You don't think I'm feminine? Suck my dick."

I came off the stage and Mitzi grabs me. "Go do twenty in the main room," she says. She took me from amateur night into the main room in the same night and that had never happened before.

I knew my six-minute act was awesome 'cause I used to win money in comedy contests with it. I'd already won the Denver laff-off with the same act. And down in the trenches, contests are hell and the competition pretty stiff. This one bar offered a hundred bucks and I really had my eye on it. However, I had to follow a sword swallower. Stuck things on fire down his throat and these drunks just loved it. And I *needed* that money for my kids. So I walk out—and it's on a disco floor with everybody around you—and I say, "That wimp? At least I swallow." I beat that guy out, won the hundred bucks. I only lost twice, one time to a four-hundred-pound belly dancer, another to a seventy-five-year-old grandma.

One night after I finished my act at the Comedy Store, this guy comes up to me and says, "Hi, Roseanne, I really love you."

"Oh, well, isn't that great. Move," I said, kinda shoving him out of the way.

"Roseanne—" the guy starts laughing. "You don't know who I am, do you?" And then I knew who he was.

He handed me his card, but every comic knew his name at that time.

"I'm Jim McCawley from 'The Tonight Show.' I want to put you on Friday. Come down and see me at NBC tomorrow."

I was just breathless. Goin' on Friday for the first shot? That's when they put on somebody that's real hot. You get booked for Wednesday, you're happy and all, but Friday—that's for somebody they think is gonna be real big. Oh, I just freaked after that. I took his card and thanked him, then walked out to the lobby where the cashiers and waitresses hung out.

"Go in there and get my sister," I ordered one of them. Geraldine, who was there for my act, came running out.

"Okay, who was he? Who was he? I know he was *someone.*" She's jumping up and down. I couldn't even talk so I just handed her the card. And then we both went nuts. You know how when you're a kid and you get excited, you do that gallop-run? We ran outside, screaming, trotting around in the middle of Sunset Boulevard, in the middle of traffic. "JESUS CHRIST, IT'S HERE! IT'S HERE!" I knew that was it. I knew right then *that was it.* We found a pay phone.

Believe it or not, the first people I called were my parents. Mom starts shouting away from the phone, "She got 'The Tonight Show'! She got 'The Tonight Show'!" Then I called Bill.

"Oh. Well ... okay. Well ... where's the Tide?" I started crying really bad. Why couldn't he be happy for me?

I was staying at this girl comic's apartment down in Santa Monica, not far from where I'm living right now. Her name was Dianne Ford and she was kind enough to put me and my kids up for the first two weeks we moved out to L.A. The kids went back to their father in Denver right after that, while I stayed and dug out a foothold for us. I was staying with Dianne again when I got the big word from Jim McCawley.

For a week before my performance I was going to the "Tonight Show" offices every day, going over my material with Jim, having the "Tonight Show" people okay it. They didn't want me to say "uterus" on the air because no one had ever used that word on TV before.

"I don't know if I can clear this show," Jim cautioned.

"There's nothing wrong with the word 'uterus,' " I told him, but he kept insisting he was gonna have trouble clearing it. In the end, "uterus" was cleared, a step in the right direction in that pretty soon these guys might even be ready to admit that we have them. Jim was actually very kind to me; he took me to comedy clubs all over town, showed me where I could work.

Just before I went out to do my six minutes on "The Tonight Show," I opened this letter I had written to myself long ago with the intention of reading it should I ever get to do "The Tonight Show." Mostly what it said was: "This is the beginning of your life, for She who is and is not yet," something I found myself writing frequently, but not understanding why or what it meant. And it also said, "This is for my kids, because my kids are gonna go to college." And then at the very end, I wrote "For Elisia." So I read this letter that had every secret thing about my hopes and dreams since I was two years old, everything I had somehow known, and it was like a heroin rush. And then Johnny introduced me:

"Here's a housewife from Denver, she's been working at the Comedy Store, a very funny young lady— please welcome Roseanne Barr." I don't remember anything after that. But luckily, I have a videotape.

As I'm walking off, Johnny says to the audience, "She's a very funny girl. *Very* funny girl."

Dianne Ford was the first woman headliner I ever saw, the first real working comic to ever comment on my act. I asked her to watch my act and critique it for me. This is what she said: "You need to lose about fifteen pounds. And your pants are way too tight. They go right up your crotch." Well, thank you, Miss Ford. That week I spent at the NBC studios, Dianne was out of town, so I had the apartment to myself, meaning housecleaning would not be a high priority. In fact, the apartment was a total pigsty. She came back into town a day early—the night that I performed on "The Tonight Show." After the taping, I was so psyched, ecstatic, jazzed, man. Using

Dianne's car, I drove to the Comedy Store to watch my-self on the show. Dianne came looking for me and it wasn't for an autograph.

"Where's my car?" she's frothing at me, while I'm thinking what the hell is she doing home a day early? It got worse when she saw the condition of her apartment. Hey, what can I say? The nesting instinct was supplanted by good timing. I didn't want to clean the room, I wanted to work it. I planned on hiring a housecleaning service for a hundred bucks to come in and undo my mess at Dianne's but she had to blow into town a day early. So I do "The Tonight Show" and I'm just higher than hell, greatest night of my life, and Dianne throws all my stuff in the street and kicks me out of her apartment. "Johnny, this is Roseanne. I'm homeless."

Second time I went on "The Tonight Show," I had about five minutes of clean jokes. Three months later, I went back on with totally unrehearsed material. I called Tom and some other guys I knew. "Christ, I don't have any clean material," I panicked. "Can you write me some jokes?"

This time, I had the jokes written on my hand. I did real well again. But then Johnny called me over to sit with him—he wanted to panel me—and I didn't have any more material. I'm outa here, I'm thinking, but Johnny keeps waving me over. I gave him another quick wave and just kept walkin'—got the hell outa there. Third time on the show, they nailed me. "You're gonna panel after your act," they let me know, in no uncertain terms. I got a reprieve at the last minute when they called it off, claiming there wasn't enough time. Thank God. So I'm in my dressing room, unwinding, coming back. Knock-knock. "Get out there. Johnny wants you."

I went out there without a damn thing to say except, "Thank you, Mr. Carson. Thank you. I'll never be able to thank you. I appreciate everything." I kept saying that about five thousand times until he just cut me off. I was a babbling idiot. The only saving grace was that comics were always last, or second to the last, to come out. Johnny knows his stuff. He still knows how to do it. And he made all of us comics . . . imagine what I felt like when he came backstage, took my hand and said, "Do you write your own material?" (I told him I did.) "You have great timing." I thanked him effusively. He was patting my hand. "You're going to be a big star, maybe the biggest woman comic ever. I PERSONALLY GUARANTEE IT." Seeing him some years later backstage at Bob Hope's ninetieth birthday bash, and hearing him say he felt rusty because he hadn't worked in a while, was so overwhelming to me. Johnny Carson, comic. Comics are the greatest damn people on earth, never really too secure. In the end, all the best things to do in life usually end up in humiliation, arrest, or nudity, anyway.

A ROUND OF HOLLYWOOD BUNGALOWS FOR EVERYONE

I moved to Los Angeles with the kids while Bill stayed in Denver to sell the house. We rented a place at the bottom of Laurel Canyon, in West Hollywood, the hugest gay area in the world, a happening area, but not a good place to have kids. And I have the noisiest kids on earth. People would come down every day and stand under my window, screaming "KEEP THOSE KIDS QUIET!" To add to the mix, my sisters were living with me too.

And as usual, some part of that family was always in a state of crisis and I, being the shit-storm custodian, was the first to hear about it. Stephanie had followed her new boyfriend to San Diego and had been living with him for a year there when I visited her. Mitzi Shore had another comedy club in La Jolla and while I was booked there, I made the short trip to San Diego to see Steph. And her arm was broken.

When I asked Steph who broke her arm, she told me her boyfriend did it.

"That's it, you're going back there, you're getting your stuff, you're gone, you're leaving."

"I can't," she cried, standing there with her fucking arm covered with plaster. I said, "Yes you can. Look, I've helped you out before, come and got you, and I'm here now. But if you don't get your stuff right this minute and come with me right now, I'm not going to come back for you again. You need to get out of there."

Steph came up to L.A. this time, joining Geraldine and me and my kids until Bill could sell our house in Denver and join me.

Work. Thanks to Mitzi Shore, who told me she would take care of me if I moved to L.A., booking me in Vegas once a month. So I made about two thousand bucks a month, which was all I needed. And then Bill showed up. When comedy was my Monday-night little hobby, it was okay. But when things started to get big for me, he had nothing but resentment. The night he came out to L.A., we sat out on the front porch.

"Isn't this great?" I said, and I meant it, 'cause things were happening for me.

"Well, you know what? It's *not* great. And you're gonna have to give me some time to get used to it," Bill hissed back. And there was a lot to get used to: not having to work, not having to worry about money. All he was expected to do was take care of the kids while I toured, which was evidently too much to ask. Only now, after years of therapy, are the kids beginning to recover from Bill's parenting. Bill was so drunk sometimes that he couldn't send them to school because he couldn't get out of bed.

My career, then, was off and running. My personal life, as always, was in the crapper. At the time, I was working for a week in Las Vegas when I got this weird plan in my head.

I called everybody in the family. I wanted all of them to come to Las Vegas for a big confrontation, hoping to resolve the whole incest issue between Dad and Steph once and for all. Was there some other reason behind my summit meeting? What was there that I, not consciously aware of at the time, was following, tracking down, circling like a bird dog, all instinct and nerves? Tragedy, according to Aristotle (Mister Earth, Wind, and Fire), occurs when the pursuit of the truth results in the seeker's demise. The closer I got, the further away I was, this time in Las Vegas.

"Well, we don't believe her," my brother, Ben, referring again to our dear old dad's molestation of Steph and serving as official spokesperson, told me.

"You know what? It doesn't matter if you all believe it or not," I told him. "Because *she* believes it and we have to deal with it. *She believes it*, so deal with that." And that kind of got through, kinda like a crisis by default. The family had been torn apart for almost five years now over this issue and over Mom's refusal to deal with it. I got everyone to finally admit that we had a *problem*. Progress.

So it's the Barrs in Las Vegas. We were all in the same suite, which of course I paid for, along with the plane tickets. Steph listed the things Daddy did to her, and that she wanted him to take responsibility for doing them. At that point my mother, sitting on the bed rocking, kept saying, "Don't do this, don't do this." And my dad said, "Helen, shut up. I can handle it, so shut up. I take the responsibility for it. But I was just playing around, I didn't mean anything by it. Maybe it was inappropriate and I imagine it was, but . . . this is just a misunderstanding. I meant it to be funny."

So now everything was going to be just hunky-dory because this was just a misunderstanding, just miscommunication. This was how we could finally settle it in our heads. That Daddy would take responsibility for what happened, but it wasn't really his fault because he was meaning to be funny.

And at the time, even to me, that seemed to put an end to it 'cause he was always doing things to be funny. And I thought they were funny then. Funny and gross. Funny and gross and vaguely threatening, and we always laughed it off. Like him laying in front of the TV with his hand in his underpants playing with his penis all night for hours and hours. We'd sit there on the couch and hoot at him with our mom there. "Dad, get your hand out of your pants, you pig." He'd chase us all over the room, trying to make us smell his fingers. Then he'd go back in front of the TV and do his thing some more, always playing with himself. My mother never said, "You know it's just not appropriate for you to do that in front of your children." A laff riot.

Later she would deny that she was abused, but I know the same thing jelled in Steph's mind, too. It was like, okay, it was over, he admitted everything, it was inappropriate, he shouldn't have done it, shouldn't've laid on top of her and put his hand down her pants. From the time she was four, Steph called Dad an "incestuous dog." She'd say, "Stop it, you incestuous dog." We'd all laugh. But years later, as she approached womanhood—seventeen years old—he got on top of her and stuck his hands down her pants, he looked her right in the eye, right on top of her, and slurred, "You incestuous dog." This time it was different. This time it wasn't funny at all. This time it scared her enough for her to take her Bat Mitzvah money and run away to Denver.

But now everything was wonderful once more. We all got real close there in Las Vegas.

About every three weeks after our big powwow my parents would come out without notice and show up at my door, expecting to live with us for a week or two. We had a guest house. Of course my two sisters lived in it but my parents would go back there and stay with them—a one-room guest house. Bill finally freaked out.

"You have to tell your parents not to come here anymore without being invited, and with no notice," he said. I called my mother into the kitchen.

"Mom, you guys are going to have to call first and not just show up out here and you can't come out every two or three weeks anymore. My husband says he doesn't like it, you know, when you guys come out with no notice, every few weeks, and then stay for weeks. He doesn't want that to happen anymore," I told her. With tears welling in her eyes (which she can do *so* easily. She always cries. Everything makes her cry), her voice breaking, she cried in a little baby-girl voice, "I thought you *liked* us." That was another time that I looked at her and saw the manipulator she really was with her baby thing.

"Talk to me when you're ready to talk to me like an adult. I'm not going to take this shit," I said, and she shuffled out of the kitchen like she was on her way to a firing squad. She came back about a half hour later still crying.

"We understand." She was stoic now, implying

through her behavior that I had no idea of how horrible a bitch I was. Never mind their violations of my family and my space. "And we aren't going to come at all anymore until you invite us." The intention here was to bury me so deep in guilt you'd need a steam shovel to find me.

From that point on, somebody's comedy got louder, somebody's life more lurid, somebody's secret less vaulted.

AGENTS
OF ORANGE

The first time that I was on "The Tonight Show," I did my bit, got my cheers, then walked behind the curtain. There was a hall full of managers and agents. At first I thought, well, this must be what it's like when any comic goes on. I found out later, it isn't. It's only when Jim McCawley thinks that somebody's gonna be real big. He pounds the drums, beats the tomtoms, and you've got scalp hunters and fur traders everywhere. I come down the hall and I'm swarmed by these folks as if I'm Marilyn Monroe gushing, "We want to represent you." I'd been in L.A. for a week and I had no idea who was good or what to think.

"Who should I have lunch with?" I asked Jim. There must've been twenty agents there; any time you get over ten of them in a room, you get real scared cuz lips move over perfect teeth and no sounds come out.

"If you're gonna have lunch with anybody, have lunch with this one guy because he manages Sylvester Stallone," Jim told me.

Enter Herby Nanas, my fast-talking Hollywood manager and the first in a long line of people I fired. Carsey-Werner tried to call me for over a year. Herby, my protector, said, "We're gonna own our *own* show." Excellent thinking, but the timing was all wrong. You don't hire a chef, waitresses, and a hostess if you're still operating a wiener wagon. You don't run the Gulf War if you're Kuwait. But Herby insisted that we'd cut our own deal with the network, and we wouldn't be working for anybody.

"None of the networks are interested in you just yet," Herby insisted. "You'll have to go out on tour again and build up some heat," he said, making his pitch for control. I knew I would never leave my kids alone again after the Julio Iglesias tour Herby booked me on for eighteen weeks. I took some time out to smoke a joint and read my tarot cards, which were never wrong. And they weren't this time, either. The thing about the cards, really, is that they guide your unconscious to help you focus in.

You already know all the answers you need. It's just a tool to help you bring them up.

I had listened to and trusted Herby—like a lot of other folks in this town—and it took me a while to figure this out: No one knew more than me, or better than me what to do WITH ME.

Herby was always trying to steer me into the Erma Bombeck thing.

"You can't say 'fuck' anymore," he'd insist. "You can't say 'Suck my dick.' People will think you're a *cunt*." Oh, that Herby.

"Keep it clean, keep it clean. You're gonna have a much bigger career," he kept telling me while we were filming the first HBO special. I was pretty torn because to me, I had already cleaned it up a lot. Once, when I was in Atlantic City, opening for Andy Williams in '87, Herby admonished me again.

"Honey, stay a lady. A LADY. A LADY. A LADY." Well, all I can say is I tried. To mix psychobabble metaphors, my superego kept telling me that Herby knew best while my reptilian complex wanted to breathe fire. The voice kept saying no, nobody knows anything but you. Do what *you* want.

There were a lot of old people in the audience who weren't getting any of the jokes. They had that look of hidden incontinence on their faces, the look that said, Oh, my God, what is she saying? She's supposed to be doing look-how-fat-I-am jokes, like I'm the big victim.

I talked to Loretta Lynn about that one time. She told me, "Honey, when I started singing, they was all singin' 'Don't leave me, don't break my heart' stuff. I came in there and it was 'I've got the Pill now, you old goat.' " She was my idol. I used to listen to her and think "how do I put that into stand-up?" Or like Richard Pryor, who gets into the stereotype and blows it up from the inside. He just imbues it with humanity and it crumbles. So these are some of the reptilian voices calling to me while I'm on stage in Atlantic City. I'm doing these husband jokes. I call out to a woman in the audience: "How long you been married? Does he drive you crazy or what?" This is an old Jewish people crowd and their parents. The woman yells back:

"No! We're very happy! What's a matter? Are ya jealous?" I saw Herby standing near the curtain out of the corner of my eye. He's got this pleading "Please behave" look, and he's gesturing with his hands, the way a third-base coach tells you to go in to home plate sliding.

"Why would I be jealous of you, lady?" I said. "I got a long time to live." Makin' squares laugh . . . I guess I just couldn't be nice. They all booed while Herby swooned and fell against the curtain like he's just suffered a coronary. Herby had that, "Your career is over" look all over him again.

After returning to L.A. from Atlantic City, I called a meeting with all my advisors—my publicist, Herby, and my agents.

"I want you all to tell me what I could do right now to totally screw up my career," I said. "Is there anything I could do to end it, to totally fuck it up for good?" One thing that I always knew from my mysticism days was as soon as you figure out the right question to ask, people *want* to tell you the answer, if they know it. They *have* to tell you. People *can't* not tell you if you have the right words in the right sequence. If you have the language reversed and the latchkey words out of order, they'll beg off or tell you it's none of your business. Since these people perceive themselves as being essentially helpful (which was always one of the blackest ironies this side of the fault lines), they are all quick to reply, ready with a constructive word, chirping to outdo each other in the minting of wisdom.

"Yes," they reply. "You could begin to talk about your political and religious beliefs." They all knew that I had a certain voice in me, knew especially how abrasive it was, and were always on the lookout for evidence of it, so it could be erased.

"Thank you," I dismissed them. Then I got on the phone to *The New York Times* and whoever else would listen and spouted off every sociopolitical and religious argument (all of them blasphemous) I could recall. I did this not to destroy myself, but knowing how limited the collective thought of my brain trust of advisors was, I acted with glee, for they had given me the key to a whole new career, closer to the one I had first imagined. If they had thought of it, it was like giving a terrorist a hand grenade. Every interview I gave from then on, I'd say how serious I was about my feminist beliefs. And depending on how you looked at it, in my latest effort (to self-destruct, as they say), my work suffered/ soared, too.

The next Big Thing I did was go to my agents (who were then at TRIAD), whom Herby always dealt with for me—and I told them I wanted to meet with TV producers. I met with Norman Lear first. Norman really liked me and was interested in doing something. "You're gonna be bigger than 'Mary Hartman,'" he swore. I liked Norman back, always loved his shows but my feeling was if I go with him, I'll never entirely have what I want, which was control of my own show. Hey, I was out there to take over the whole town, right? RIGHT? I met with a few others, then finally met with Carsey-Werner. Carsey-Werner had Mister Cosby. And I knew *he* ran his show. It was his vision.

"I don't wanna work with you no more," I told Herby over the phone.

"Honey, can we talk about this?" I said no and I hung up. I had made that same call in my mind about a million times before then.

After I fired Herby, I met the next day with Marcy Carsey. Both of us were silent for a few seconds.

"You wanna do a show?" she finally asked.

"I wanna do it," I told her. "Let's do it—NOW."

BACK TO THE MATT

People have the power
to dream/to rule
to wrestle the earth from fools.
—FRED SMITH AND PATTI SMITH

So, I'm in the trailer, it's about the fourth show. Instead of cooling down after the Great Bed Confrontation, my war with Matt & Co. just got hotter. To jack myself up, every day I listened to Patti Smith sing "People Have the Power." I put that song on a hundred and fifty times per day.

Soon the theater of battle spread into newsprint; from my point of view, I couldn't have been more happy. They were eviscerating my show, goddamnit, they were

Osterizing it into the pastel purée that had been spread over the networks for too long now, the same unsatisfying, tasteless, colorless (forget odorless—it stunk) polenta of sitcoms that I couldn't stomach.

I related all of this and more in an interview with *The New York Times,* the more being the fact that I labeled Matt an idiot and a lousy writer to boot. Matt did his own *Time* piece, but did more damage bludgeoning the show: more castration jokes, more idiotic mugging, making the Dan character bigger while whittling my role down, smaller and smaller.

The fourth show: during one of our meetings (I would've preferred a barium enema and two hours of shitting pink to these meetings, but the show must go on), Matt, being a natural-born storyteller, harkens back to his Cosby days:

"You know, Cosby was a five-hundred-pound gorilla. *He* wouldn't do what I wanted him to. I should've known then. He's a five-hundred-pound gorilla and he sits wherever he wants to."

"Well, you oughta be kissing his ass that you were allowed to write on his show because you're such a hack, Matt." After the meeting, my sister Geraldine whispers to me, "You think he knows he just met the two-thousand-pound gorilla?"

"No. No, he doesn't see it because I'm a woman." Luckily. I was glad he didn't see it because in severely un-

derestimating what I was capable of doing, Matt provided me with duty-free passage. And I knew already
what I was gonna do.

"Get that SOB out of here now. I'm not working with
him no more." I was sitting in Marcy Carsey's office. She
and Tom Werner were calmly listening to me rail on
about Matt. Using bad language and blue-collar syntax
was more than just a habit with me (aside from being
purely political—I love Woody Guthrie). I wanted to see
if I could get these people to flinch, to act out of character, out of the cool, unflappable force field they worked
so hard to project, the way really spoiled teenagers tried
to act like sophisticated adults in the fifties.

  "Well, Roseanne, he's got a contract for thirteen episodes," Marcy tried to Pontius Pilate her way out of any
responsibility.

  "If you can just make it to thirteen, we'll replace
him," Tom Werner reasoned, his forbearance and indul-
gence utterly complete and unassailable, "but we need
that time to find somebody else." Blah blah blah. It was
all fat-mouth, Hollywood horse pucky, but all the same,
I went for it.

  "Okay, I understand. I don't want to do anything
that will harm or jeopardize the show. I will work with
him until thirteen—"

"Good. Gre-eeatt," Tom Werner stretched the word out insincerely, as though he'd just been told a distant relative had come to sleep on his couch for the next month.

"—but in the meantime you gotta get somebody in the middle to come and give me his notes."

"See? Deep down you really do want to work with him—"

"No. I want somebody to bring me his notes because I don't want to see him, I don't want him touching me, I don't want to sit in a room with him, and I sure as hell don't want to talk to him—ever, ever again." Deep down I wanted to force-feed him his own body, piece by maggot-infested piece.

Danny Jacobson was brought in as my liaison to Matt Williams. I liked him because he was one of the only people walking the set who didn't go to college with Matt. "Hurry up and get good," I told him, "because I'm gonna make you the head writer." Danny helped me get through the thirteen episodes, however, with my brainpan relatively lithium-free. I would make changes when I wanted to and fax them to Matt, who seemed to have no idea that after the thirteenth show was in the can, so was he. By now I was rewriting everything and naturally not getting the credit for it. I got comfortable with Danny, a major mistake because that whole time Danny seemed to be working only for himself.

There was one guy, however, who knew my character, knew her voice, and even knew a little bit about me and where I came from, or at least could stand in the same room with me without the sweat of his insincerity melting the very microfibers of his pants. By that time, I was doing much of my own writing and I needed some help with the workload.

LOVE AMONG THE RUINS

I promised Tom Arnold a job with the show and he moved out to L.A. in 1988 for that reason. His agent called, just after he arrived in L.A., asking about the job writing for the show. I stalled and made up excuses.

"Well, I'm ready to go to work for the show," Tom told me in that joking way of his that means he's not joking.

"Don't worry, it'll happen," I assured him. "I'm working on them."

After the pilot for the show had been shot, it was

time to hire writers to work through the summer on the episodes. To keep himself available to write for the show, Tom didn't take any stand-up bookings for that summer. Much later, Tom told me what kind of hell he was going through, waiting for the big call. "Man, if she wanted to, she could get you a job just like that if she wanted you to be a writer on the show," Tom's manager scoffed, humiliating him enough to call me from his parents' cottage, late that summer.

"How you doing?" Tom began.

"Where the hell have you been?" The best defense and all that shit.

"Playing the fucking Sands Hotel with Frank, Sammy, and Liza. So when's the show start, Rosey? I'm ready to go."

"The writers have already started, actually."

"Uh-huh. I know one writer who hasn't."

"Look, Tom . . . the writer thing's gonna take a little longer than I thought. But we're looking for somebody to warm up the audiences at the tapings. I want you to come and warm up the audiences."

"You're shitting me. *ME?* Wow, that's just the nicest gesture anyone's done for me since I had my stereo ripped off. Making arthritic tourists with knockoff Gucci bags and bad hearing laugh. Wow, thank you."

Tom came out, did a couple of warm-ups, and sucked. They fired him (Arlyne, my manager, did the honors) after a few more, which was just as well because he hated it. Out of a job, the last thing he wanted to hear was his manager insisting that I could land Tom a job at the mere drop of a few four-letter words. "She's supposed to be your friend—man, this is fucked up. She's your friend and she says she's got a job for you writing for the show. The show's doing great. Let me tell you something—she can get you a job right now."

Tom sent me this letter about writing for the show. "Listen, I don't know how it works out here," he wrote, "but I did move out to do this writing job and I know I'm a good writer and I can write for you. But, I can't even be friends with you if you don't keep your word on this. This is just unbelievable. I'm in shock about it."

The whole idea of putting our friendship on the line for a job devastated me; in the fullness of my self-pity there was no room for legitimate countercharges stemming from the basic decency of giving someone a job after you've led them to believe that they have one (not to mention having them schlepp across seven states to get it). After weeks of chasing my own tail over Tom, hating him for being a principled prick, hating Bill for being a superhero of compassion at home ("By God, before Tom Arnold's a writer for the show I'm gonna be a writer!"), missing Tom's comic perseverance in the face of life's stupid little injustices, the way he'd jiggle his knees when he thought he got off a good one, missing all those patient little asides he makes in lieu of sticking an ax between some asshole's shoulder blades—I broke down and called him and asked him to meet me at this delicatessen—there's no better neutral territory than to be among food, even though you wind up being a casualty of salamis and whitefish—call it friendly fire. Tom found me in the parking lot, crying in my car.

"I don't know what's happening to me," I broke down. "They're just fucking me over so bad, I can't do anything." I just let loose with the truth about my family, my kids, my work, my husband, and my life. The truth swam in the air between us and the neon deli sign. We looked at each other a long, long time. Tom broke down. He said that he would be there for me all the way, as my best friend, and that he would look for another job.

He was trying to get in shape and not be in the bars so much. There wasn't much to do in the way of hanging out, except barhopping and going to the comedy clubs—and because we'd been thrown out of so many of them, the pickin's were pretty slim. What we *could* do was take walks together, which we did a lot of, particularly while I was conducting war on the gelatinous Matt Williams and the network. We'd walk through Balboa Park, in the valley. Bill walked with us on occasion, as did Tom's finacée, Denise; eventually, it was just me and Tom. Ever helpful Bill kept saying, "You guys shouldn't walk together because the *Enquirer* will eventually find you and take pictures. I know they're looking for you."

"How do you know?" Tom asked him. Bill scribbled something on a piece of paper and handed it to him.

"Here's the guy's number." Helpful Bill.

By the winter of 1988, the powers that be were running out of excuses not to hire Tom and began walking the other way when they'd hear me coming in the halls, knowing I'd be getting in their veiny, reticulated faces about Tom working for the show. Whereas my husband was snuggling up to the garbage trollers at the *National Enquirer*, Arlyne was secretly washing dishes (I was the dirty plate) and planning her own career. As a strategist she could be brilliant; the problem was she never did it for me, but for herself.

In order to keep Tom off the show, as a diversionary maneuver, Arlyne signed him to a fifteen-thousand-dollar contract to write my act for my HBO special. Tom was pleased, but still pressed Arlyne about writing for my show—that was the carrot in front of the ole geezer for him.

As I say, he knew my character better than anyone except me, and even that is up to interpretation. He'd been writing jokes for my urban guerrilla fighter housewife since 1983 and in some ways was my personal chronicler. He had a remarkable memory (mine had been systematically dismantled, neuron by neuron, by the concentration camp they called home), and his knack for details would help me recall incidents that had been long ago stowed away in vacant gray matter—stuff from our days on the road, in the clubs. Also, Tom had been the prototype I used for the Dan Conner character. He knew the characters, watched all of them age, grow, intermingle, fail, succeed, and connect—he knew the show better than he knew the meat-packing plant, and he knew that place pretty damn well. And he sure knew the show better than Matt. So Tom asked Arlyne for an answer on the show.

"You'll be too busy writing the special to write on the show. I don't think you can handle both. No one could." Arlyne was in her reasonable mode.

"Sure I can."

"But you haven't written a script yet, Tom. You need to write a script if you want to write for the show. When will you have time for that?"

"I'll have it for you on Monday," Tom assured her. "And if I do, I'm on the show, right?"

"Guaranteed." Arlyne smiled. She had reason to be happy. It was Friday.

Over that weekend, Tom wrote this extraordinary script—we still use pieces or bits from it all the time. He wrote a dog into the script and the story centered around the dog dying and everyone's different impressions of the dog and what it meant to them. After reading Tom's script Arlyne called him into her office late Monday afternoon.

"Don't you ever watch the show?" Arlyne started. Tom said that for the first time he noticed the shape of her eyes looked like the slots where you shove quarters into parking meters.

"Yeah, sure. All the time. Why?"

"There's no dog."

"Excuse me?"

"You have a dog in your script. There's no dog on the show."

"Well, yeah, there isn't *now*. But the show's gonna be on for a few more years. Maybe there would be a dog. There could be a dog in the future. Right?"

"Well, I think you better just watch the show and stick to writing jokes." Arlyne frowned, glancing at the door, insinuating that he should use it. Then she paid more attention to the lint on her lapel than to Tom. So much for guaranteed.

"I want you to hire Tom Arnold to help me write the show. He knows my character and my voice. He's been writing for me for six years," I told Matt, who routinely refused to hire him again. I know now that if you want to, you can hire twenty goddamn writers for your show.

"He's never written for TV before."

That was the excuse Matt gave for not hiring Tom, conveniently forgetting that none of the Dristan-sniffing college buddies he hired as writers had any TV experience, either. Matt wouldn't hire Tom. He needed to keep me isolated and in Tom, I might find an ally. I liked Tom and what I liked, needless to say, was not high on Matt's "things to do" list. But on that old fart's list, I was top dog.

Sunday, February 12, 1989: The Grateful Dead were coming to town!

"I'll get the tickets," Tom told me. When he showed up, he didn't have them. But he had the pot.

In the car, we fought.

"Well, how are we gonna get in, Tom? Damn! Why didn't you go to Ticketron?"

"Because I don't have a car, remember? Just mellow out. I'll get us tickets when we get there."

"It's a sellout."

"I'll get us tickets, okay?" I wanted to ask him just how the hell he planned on accomplishing that, since the concert was a sellout, but I soon found out how.

"ROSEANNE BARR NEEDS TWO TICKETS! ROSEANNE BARR NEEDS TWO TICKETS!" Tom shouted in front of the Forum and damned if we didn't get great seats.

Once inside we smoked a bale of pot, sang along to "Casey Jones," and got blown away by the plaintive, jangly music, at once lonesome and funny. Wrapped in the liquidy, moving cocoon of the high, we talked and talked about the show and everything else, kind of circling the block, passing the place that housed our feelings for each other a few times before we dared go in.

"See? Didn't I tell you things would turn out great?" Tom hollered in my ear.

"Yeah . . . this is so cool . . ." I said, ripped to the

rafters. "This is so much fun, Bill would never do this with me."

Tom said, "Denise, either."

"Bill and Denise," Tom added. "Maybe we could just sort of introduce them to each other, or just have them killed, then we could have fun all the time." We laughed and laughed.

"I'm sorry I bitched at you about not having tickets," I said. "Sometimes I don't even know how you could even like me."

"Like ya?" I remember a beat or two, here. Then very quietly spoken: "I love you." Then, "and you love me, too." And for an instant everything went still, like someone just said E. F. Hutton; he said it in the manner of children who, knowing they're gonna get in trouble for what they say, have to say it anyway.

"You're always taking care of everybody but I know what you really need is to be taken care of," he said. "And everybody's always taking care of me, but what I really need is to take care of somebody else."

I hurriedly excused myself for the bathroom, where I sat and cried, feeling horrible elation and wonderful fear. *Somebody really really loves me.* I felt silent and small.

I drove Tom back to his apartment in Van Nuys that night. I told him everything—about Bill, about how unhappy I was. I told him how much I loved my kids and that I wanted them to be okay, even if their father did have a brain the size of a lake perch's and saw life's complexities in terms of different zip codes.

"Look—I gotta tell you something," Tom reluctantly began, and it was like, aha, the Mary Jane's wearing off and he's about to have a stroke after remembering what he said at the (fabulous) Forum. "I haven't told you this because I didn't want to say anything against Bill. But here's the deal. He's been calling Matt Williams all fall, telling him how you're crazy. He is always telling me: 'Rosey's insane, violent, crazy, and I already have a divorce lawyer waiting in the wings,' and how he's just hanging on for residuals. Sorry, but that just doesn't sound like a guy who loves you too much. There. I said it."

There were calls coming in that night, on Tom's answering machine, from both Bill and Denise. We waited until the messages played through (out of reverence for the soon-to-be-departed?) and then hugged. The hug might have led to some tentative kissing but we both sensibly agreed that if we started something, we might never stop, or some such teenage love story. At the door, though, Tom asked me if I'd at least think about getting a divorce. What he lacked in tact, he made up for in tenacity. In spades. And at that moment, he was the wholest, most fleshed-out, most real person I knew. And I knew some real doozies.

The end of the thirteenth episode: To me, it should've been declared a national holiday. I felt liberated and free, God Almighty, I felt free, free from the oppression of battle-ax jokes, free from reconnaissance, spying, free from the five-month psychological gang bang I'd been through. And where he was going, Matt would need an arm as long as the fucking Golden Gate Bridge in order to get his soiled fingers in my back. To the moon, Matt!

But *nothing happened*. Matt was still there, pumping out comedy fit for a king. "Here, King" if the king liked to watch "Three's Company" and "Who's the Boss?"

"Who have you gotten to replace Matt?" I think I might've said hello first, not that it mattered to Carsey and Werner. They were lost in fast-file phase, mentally reviewing lame excuses at the speed of light.

"We . . . just haven't been able to find anybody yet," said Marcy, in a way that a better person (read: sucker) would've actually felt sorry for her, instead of me.

"What? What the hell do you mean you haven't found anyone yet? How many months have you had?"

"Well, Roseanne, we just don't think anybody can write the show as well as Matt."

I left their office with my ears as red as a clown's nose, which was all the same anyway, since I was due in wardrobe and lately they'd been dressing me like a circus

pony. Ha-ha, the joke's on Roseanne—just more castration jokes courtesy of Matt Williams, your sitcom demo-
lition expert. I gotta say the wardrobe business was
pissing me off a little more than usual.

They had me looking like a fat-lady circus clown,
with aprons and frilly garbage, like some Norwegian version of "Hee Haw." Matt, of course, was the mastermind,
but his "Uncle Woman," as in "Uncle Tom,"* was this
middle-aged dumb bitch—Miss Hathaway, I called her—
who served as his assistant producer. At the height of my
schism with Matt, Miss Hathaway had gone to the wardrobe people to impart Matt's clown-suit edict. One of the
wardrobe girls told her that I wasn't gonna like the outfits
she had picked out. "I don't care what *Roseanne* likes.
This is the nature of the show," Miss Hathaway sniffed.

So now they had a divining rod that helped them lo-
cate the nature of the show and they all knew what
"working-class" meant. This was their idea of working-
class: They were up there in the production office in what
I called "the big house," on my money, eating broccoli
and asparagus and rare steaks for lunch while we had a
bowl of potato chips and some M & Ms. And they knew
what working-class meant. My ass. They didn't know
what working was and they sure as hell had no idea what
class was, neither.

*A woman whose first order is to be a lackey to anti-woman
males.

I spent Valentine's Day with Tom, while my husband was huddled by himself somewhere, fantasizing how he was gonna spend all that alimony money he figured he'd be raking in.

Tom was sweet. Both of us were nervous as hell about the prospect of sex, as though we had both never flown in an airplane before. We got into some extremely heavy hugging, then took the edge off with some killer Hawaiian pot that, after two hits, made you feel like you had powers of levitation and you could bend forks with your mind. About the time the universe started to collapse into itself and get smaller, falling, swallowing whole galaxies, whole star clusters, whole planetary systems, whole civilizations—all peoples, including Christine Lunde's hair, pets and pests alike, buildings, cars, trains, Burger Kings, health spas, shoehorns, speculums, those little scooper things that make cantaloupe balls, those little plastic tags that say "Key buy" at Von's—all of it gone, until only one sentence remains in existence—one big sentence and before I can read what it says, there's a knock at the door. Tom was too stoned to get up so I dragged myself across the room. When I got to the door, I scanned the whole slab for the little peephole but it was gone. I thought I might've shrunk and tried standing on my tiptoes and it was still gone. I thought I might've grown and bent low, running my hands over the place where I thought the peephole should be. But it wasn't there.

"We're at *my* house, Rosey," Tom called out from under his arms, his head cradled between both of them, on the table. "No peephole." I opened the door and there was this man from the *National Enquirer* standing there. He had this English accent that made him sound like a drag queen doing Maggie Smith.

"Roseahnn—when ahre yew gawing to leave Bill ahnd mahry Toam?" I screamed and slammed the door on him. A half hour later, when I left to go home, still stoned on my ass, he was still there, waiting.

"Rrroseahnn. Can you tell me now when ahre yew gawing to leave Bill ahnd mahry Toam Ahnald?"

QUEEN

The wardrobe girl came down to visit me. Upset and agitated, she wouldn't stay long enough to sit down.

"I'm probably gonna get into all kinds of trouble for telling you this, but we've been told not to listen to anything you say." Stuck with Matt Williams in a show that used my name but was no longer about me and forced to wear circus pony outfits, suddenly I needed a scissors real bad. When I found a decent one—nice *long* blades—I took it down to Miss Hathaway's office, and took a little meeting with Miss Hathaway. Did I have a bone to pick?

"Bitch, if you ever, ever tell anybody not to listen to me again, you know what I'm gonna do? I'm gonna take this scissors and cut your eyes out and stab you to death." Then I left. 'Cause one more minute with her and I probably would've done it (I was into a *West Side Story* thing at the time, if that at all helps). She came running out of her office, trailing me down the hall.

"Roseanne! Can we talk about this? Can we have lunch?"

"You stay away from me, you old whore, or I'll cut you, so help me!" I whirled around and shooed her off. I had one other stop to make before that day was over and some blithering hedgehog with matching purse and shoes pestering me about lunch after I threatened to cut her a couple of new eye sockets wasn't gonna hold me up.

"I'm done. I'm not gonna take it no more," I told Carsey and Werner. "I'm not gonna listen to you promise me shit anymore. I did what I said I was gonna do. You know and I know that I worked with that little ignorant arrogant ijjit for thirteen shows and took it up the butt, in the mouth, up the nose, and in the ear and still held still, damnit. I'm gone."

Then I made the same low-key speech at the network, which produced a lot of head-shaking and shoulder-shrugging, then that inevitable line about messing up my career forever, self-destructing, being blackballed and shamed and ostracized. Well, I didn't give a flying fuck. I'd been poor before and I do poor really well. I'll be poor again. Once I built a railroad and now it's gone; brother can you spare a dime? My loving husband, Bill, as loyal as a salmon in a spawning pool, Bill, the spouse who thought exchanging vows meant you could trade up, meanwhile was talking to everyone but me, including Tom.

"Listen, I just got off the phone with Matt Williams, who's been fighting tooth and nail with Rosey. I told him, Matt, man, look, Rosey's crazy. Just bear with us, okay. She's throwing it all away, Tom. She's throwing away twenty-five million dollars—she is just throwing it all away—all the work everyone's done and she's just throwing it all away."

Hell, after that, how could I disappoint him? So I left. I told my husband, called all my friends, told them what I'd done, called Tom—said I'm done—I'll just do stand-up—I could do a million things, anything I wanted to do. Not that I didn't go to bed at night feeling like a castaway, like that poor sap in *2001: A Space Odyssey* who gets cut loose in deep space by that velour-voiced HAL (Matt?) computer.

Meanwhile, the network went to John Goodman and asked him if he'd take over the show if I was really gone. John, bless his size triple-x heart, refused; Laurie said she'd walk, too. The network, as it turned out, didn't have a show. John and Laurie said no way because they saw me fight every day, and I'd tell them every day what the hell was going on because *they* hated the writing, too.

"Fuck, what have we got ourselves into—this is the end of our careers," everyone fretted—it was two days before I made the big jump from the corral.

"No, it isn't gonna go down that way. I'm gonna take care of it," I swore.

John tried to sound encouraging, but with those big, droopy eyes flying at half-mast, well, let's just say I got the feeling he was reading future headlines in his head, like BOTTOM DROPS OUT, ROSEANNE SWINGS. People were saying I was crazy, looking at me like I had grown a major pair of horns, but I didn't really give a damn anymore and that was greatly exhilarating. I'll never let myself forget it.

My AWOL lasted one weekend. There's a chance I might've been just a tad disingenuous about leaving—the show was number five and moving up, soon to be number three. And we were getting a lot of press. People didn't quite get what the show was yet, but they were hinting. "Something different" was the critics' assessment du jour. I'd done a passel of interviews saying I'm not coming back, they messed me up too much, I have no pride left, I can't do my show, which had to impact on the way certain network executives were sleeping at night. They couldn't let me go because they really cared about how they looked. Nothing on the grizzled face of the planet matters more to them—apart from a primo table at the Monkey Bar or whatever watering hole is happening at the time—than how they look. So I kind of knew I'd be back somehow, but if anybody sleepwalked through a lost weekend, it was me. I upped my coffin-nail intake to four packs a day, ate like my life depended on fitting into a size twenty-six, and waited—and did a lot of tricks with cards, bones, and mirrors.

Arlyne found a guy herself named Jeff Harris—from "Diff'rent Strokes"—an old friend who could do the job—she said. Anyone, anything would be better than Matt, so I jumped at Jeff.

Hollywood is the only place on earth that has more vampires, more undead, more resurrections than a month of Easter Sundays. Matt, however, was finally gone. Halla-badabam-bada-bing.

This is how elated I was that Matt was gone and how determined I was to keep it that way: Jeff Harris was the first and only person I interviewed to replace Matt.

"You got the job," I told Jeff. "The first thing I want you to do is hire my friend Tom Arnold." Then I gave him a list of people to fire. Sorry, defending your vision is not for the squeamish.

Just after I came back, after doing the first thirteen shows, we finally got an order to do a second round, which was a huge relief for everyone. The whole atmosphere improved radically, the way things brighten up at a party after all the schmucks leave. Jeff Harris, I felt, listened to me and put what I wanted into the scripts; he gradually started to see some correct method to my madness, that I wasn't just some insane, wounded brown bear out to hack everyone to pieces and ruin everybody's day. And as far as the show goes, I was always right. I can watch any episode of my show and I can tell you how I changed it, what I put in there, and, invariably, that's the thing that anybody wrote about or remembers. If some cornball snuck in the stories, I didn't mind, as long as each show had one moment (that was all I could handle, workwise). Yeah, I wanted each show to be superior, great, but if I got one twist in that was a left turn instead of a right, in every show, I could look at myself in the mirror and say, well, okay.

Tom was about to go on the road in late March and a few weeks later, I was scheduled to start shooting a film called *She-Devil* with Meryl Streep. Call it some warped nesting instinct, or call it that stuff that went on in *An Officer and a Gentleman*—on second thought, don't call it any of that. *I wanted to mark my man territory!* Just before "Toam" was about to leave for his gala comedy tour, I showed up at his place with my sister Steph.

"Go on up and get him," I told Steph, and waited in the car. When he came down, he was shrugging like

"What gives?" I told him to get in the car, that we had something to talk about.

"I'm packing for the tour. What's up?"

"You and me are gonna go fuck." I glared at Tom and just for affect hit the automatic door locks. I wanted Tom.

We found a motel down in Encino for twenty-seven bucks a night. We didn't have any cash, so Stephanie paid for the room with her credit card. Tom was all shaky and nervous as we went up to the room.

"Well—okay, let's do it," he said, "but only because *I want to*!" We went into the room and came out about thirteen minutes later—Tom swears it was sixteen—and from then on, things just got more weird, more beautiful, more full of snafus, battles, and casualties, but with Tom by my side, the impossible thing was that everything seemed just a little less impossible. My marriage with Bill was like a close-up of tooth decay.

"Whatever you do, you gotta get me out of this marriage, even just as a friend," I appealed to Tom. "I'm in hell, it's horrible, horrible for my kids." I knew I embarrassed him (that, or he was still blushing from that two-minute offense we had in the sack) because he made some wisecrack about the decor of the room, but then he gathered me in and silently nodded. L.A. was a city and I needed a state. Tom was a state.

As we came down the stairs, Steph was looking at us as if we'd left a bomb under the bed up there.

"Did you guys have sex?"

"Well, I did," Tom said. What a guy, what a guy.

I was going to New York to do *She-Devil*. My one daughter was in the hospital and my other two kids were with Bill. The last thing I wanted him to find out while I was in New York was that I was planning on leaving him or that anything had happened between Tom and me. I was afraid he'd take it out on the kids, which later turned out to be a justifiable fear.

And you can bet a dime to the dollar that if anyone's gonna be rooting around in the smegma for something, it's gonna be the *National Enquirer*. They'd already been to Tom's apartment, asking questions. And they'd been to see Bill, the tabloid's best friend, Bill, who never heard a secret that couldn't be told. Tom called, told me the *Enquirer*'s dogging him for answers.

"They wanna know about us—what should I tell 'em? Should we just stonewall it or what?"

"However you have to do it, I don't want anyone to know because that's my kids."

Tom talked to the *Enquirer* a lot because we were trying to maintain control of the story. He told them we were friends, that we had a professional relationship, that because of the show, we were forced to spend a lot of time together. But the story began to take on a life all its own. Tom may've been real good at tricking those pigs into an oval-shaped tin can at the meat-packing plant, but to run with the bulls at the *Enquirer*, ya need a little prior experience. They have supernatural powers and ways of winding in and through you, like that liquid man in *Terminator 2*. You can pet 'em, but they bite (mainly because they're always hungry) and you gotta be careful.

The first tabloid stories were actually my parents' doing—there's a match made just south of Heaven if ever there was one, my parents and tabloids—when they were fooled by a reporter who told them he was with the London *Times*. There's a small measure of truth in this claim, like Canadians who walk around saying they're French, since the tabloid where the story ran, the *Star*, is owned by the same man who owns the London *Times*. Truth is like taffy to these people—it can be shaped into some legitimate but very sticky, protean version of reality. Impressed by the false dignity and sophistication associated with anything that has London in its title—men wearing bowlers, pumping out sterling and meaningful prose, resting only for headless kippers and tea or to adjust their stocking garters—my parents not only granted this fish 'n' chips charlatan an interview, they had him move into their house for three days for a sort of George Plimpton, *Paper Lion* kind of experience: what it's like to grow up in Roseanne's parents' home, or something like that (had he really grown up in that house, he'd either be writing for *Soldier of Fortune* magazine, or not writing at all, but holed up in a Salt Lake City motel with fourteen underage wives, claiming he was Zarathustra and biting the heads off of tree rats). They took this ringworm to din-

ner, showed him my room, showed him all my baby pictures, and let him *sleep in my goddamn bed*. Incidentally,
I learned about all of this the way everyone else did—by
reading it in the paper, since my parents never told me
about it. And the reason I read about it was because, sitting in my living room, contemplating on my good fortune with having just gotten a TV show, I got a call from
the *National Enquirer.*

"Roseanne, this is so-and-so with the *National Enquirer.* What was all this about you spending time in a
mental institution?" (My parents must've run out of baby
pictures.)

"How did you get my phone number," I demanded.

"We can get anybody's phone number, Roseanne.
Now, I understand that you spent several months in a
state mental institution."

I covered up the phone and asked Bill, who was
there in body, what I should do. I told him it was the *National Enquirer.* He told me, well, you had better talk to
them—because he was not there in mind—so I got back
on the phone and asked the caller where he got that information from. He told me he got it from my parents.
Well, about four years went by between his response and
my next word until I finally said:

"Well, I guess it's true. What do you want to know
about it?" And I started to turn into that person in me
who sort of handles everything. I said, "Actually, you
know, that was the most pleasant place I ever went to

stay in the whole state of Utah." Later on, they printed the article and it began with the headline TELEVISION'S BIG MOUTH—all that, after spilling your heart out. That's like Richard Pryor always said, "Don't be kicking my ass and yelling at me, too." After that, I had Arlyne get in touch with my parents and threaten them with their lives if they ever talked to the press again, which they never fully heeded. Of course, when I finally talked to them about it, they kind of spoke and wept at the same time, "Well, we didn't know . . ." And, of course, whenever they cry, there aren't any tears.

Eventually, all the television infotainment shows— "Hard Copy," "Inside Edition," etc.—showed up at my parents' place and surrounded the house. My parents claimed that they called the police and the cameras had to be moved back to the sidewalk, then my parents claimed they wouldn't go away, which left them no alternative but to talk to them. They gave them four stories, among them the story about me being hit by the car and how I went through a "personality change." That was my parents, that's what they always used to say to me: "You went through such a personality change." Well, Mom and Dad, I've gone through a personality change every goddamn two minutes my whole life. Ah bumped mah haid, okay?

By the time I was in New York doing *She-Devil*, Tom and I had reached a point of no return romantically. Tom's engagement to Denise was on hold. I was ready to read my Bill of Rights to Bill, although in all my mental rehearsals of the event, I'd see the light reflecting off his glasses and spirits flying out of his ears, dispatched by him to ruin me in every way. It was around this time, while I was in New York, that Tom began torching a lot of bridges. I know his heart was in the right place; it was his nose that gave him problems. "All I really expect from you is compassion and forgiveness for some of the mistakes I've made," he told me not long after this. He had this particular one in mind, to be sure, since it wound up nearly being the *Hindenburg* of our relationship.

If the tabloids "accidentally" caught us together and then did their usual ladling of the caloric, bullshit gravy, embellishing the story, it would sort of be out of our hands. In other words, the tabloids, used properly, could be my get-out-of-bad-marriage-free card. As I say, if I would've had any courage at all, I would've said, hey, Waldo, put the kegger down and listen up—you're history, I'm leaving you. But I was too scared.

Tom leaked the story that he was going to New York to see me, leaked it to one guy. There were at least fifty photographers and tabloid writers waiting at the airport when Tom landed. They followed us wherever we went, snapping pictures, those little black plastic film containers scattered in our wake, like shell casings. All of the ensuing pictures in the tabloids were fine, with enough

ambiguity in the composition so that they could be inter-
preted as, hey, just two friends hanging out, every picture
except one. The shot caught me holding two of Tom's fingers with my whole hand and by the look on my face you
could tell that we weren't together to discuss a few lines
of dialogue.

As interim executive producer, Jeff Harris didn't do much
in the way of writing. He spent most of his time playing
the piano and speaking a foreign language. I'd walk past
his office and he'd be playing the piano. I'd say hello, and
he'd answer in Spanish or Cantonese, or some damn language. He'd kind of turned the show over to Danny Jacobson, whom I was grooming for the job as head writer.
Tom was finally writing for the show then, by the way,
but they were messing with him. They never called him to
come to work—that was all because Danny Jacobson
who, I'd heard through others, kind of *liked* being in
charge. And he didn't think of Tom as anything but My
Boyfriend.

The first show that I wrote with Jeff Harris as the
head writer was the menstrual period show. I tried to
write magic into that episode—the moon, the stars, the
cycle of living things, which was all like real women's
spirituality. People still come up to me and say, hey, I
learned about my period from you—thank you. Our, *my*

daughter did, thank you. Because it was the first time that periods were talked about on prime time television without being considered above all else a curse or a drag. It was more like, now you're into the whole universe. You're a part of the cycle of life and death. I was so proud of that episode. And that's when the show started to change, to take on some meaning for me.

Women writers drive me crazy when they write from a male point of view, which they say they've had to learn to do because that's the nature of television. Well, I can't tolerate that. The most maddening thing is that most of these women have that point of view in their real lives, but they just can't seem to bring it into their writing. The problem is they're all so busy being liberated that they don't see it. They don't see that they have to be home by six to make sure there's some kind of dinner on the table or at least feel guilty about it. But, how can you be liberated when the war's still going on? There's a war going on to make sure that they will never be free—and they are participating fully in it, marching in it and calling that feminism. These people don't understand that it takes your whole life to fight for equality. Those suffragists who started the whole women's rights movement were dead for twenty years before the ERA was even proposed. So what do these people do? They devote their lives instead to some damn cause that isn't going to change a thing, like abortion laws. Who cares if it's legal or not? Learn how to give yourself and your friends abortions! The women here believe that Western women are more evolved than women from third world cultures.

If you've got an education, you have a Ph.D., then you're not like those other women, who have no rights and wear veils over their faces. They have no idea what wearing a veil is all about. And don't hand me that line about Eastern women being treated as "second-class citizens." So are *we*. We don't even have an Equal Rights Amendment. We're totally second-class citizens right down to the smallest detail. We pay twice as much as men do to have our shirts cleaned at the laundry, and it ain't 'cause they're made of silk, either. You say the women in Iran have it worse than we do. How so? They have far less rape or violence against them or their children than we do.

By now, I had no patience for anyone who didn't get it; by now, I had really become the full-blown "Queen of the Damned."

Tom, officially hired, was getting a good old-fashioned unofficial runaround. He had an idea for a story, centering—with laughable irony, now that I think of it—around me trying to get a job. There's supposed to be this big fight between me and Dan (John Goodman's character) and Tom worked the story out so there wasn't any real resolution to the problems or the big fight. "Good, good, nice, nice," the writing staff humored him. "Why don't you go home and work on it?" they suggested, which was actually not a bad idea, since they had neglected to give him an office. And it was primo strategy for them, since they really didn't want him around or taking part in any of the writers' meetings.

"How come Tom's not in the room?" I demanded one day during a story meeting. Nobody had an answer, naturally; they're all looking at each other's sanctimonious and very empty faces, including—especially—Jeff Harris. Ever see that hurt/sincere look of "I would never think of doing such a thing to you" on somebody's face? Looks kinda like a filmy slick of oil swirling over pollution-choked water, don't it? Well, there was a lot of oil in that room that day.

After a lot of searching and getting nowhere with regard to Tom's absence, one of the writers finally came to me with the answer. Jeff's reign as the benevolent Saint Francis of Assisi of Understanding just came to a quick and sorry end. The reason why Tom was not allowed in the room was because Jeff was afraid that Tom would come back to me and tell me exactly what was going on in the room. This writer had some integrity at least, and respected my talent. He smuggled a tape out of a story meeting that Tom was excluded from. Everything on it was "that stupid, big fat bitch. And keep Arnold the fuck out of here because all he is is her fucking spy." I had gone from the frying pan to the fire.

1975—Jessica and I in a photo booth. She is wearing a dress that I fashioned out of an old apron.

Christmas 1978, at my mother-in-law's house.

With Jessica in 1978.

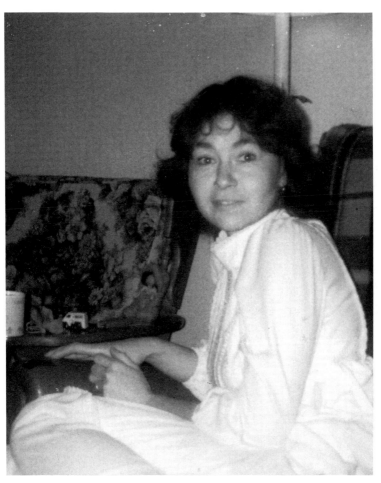

Christmas 1979. This anorexic me weighed only 103 pounds.

Here I am, still thin, right before I started stand-up (in 1980).

Here's Tom, looking good, the first year I met him. He was 23 years old!

Here I am as one of my characters—"Cece Falopia."

Laurie (Metcalf) and I in 1987 in the first Halloween show.

Sara (Gilbert) and I in 1988, when I found out that she would be leaving the show in five years to go to college.

The fourth Halloween show (1990). "How's it hangin'
Buddy?"

This was the fated dream show in 1989 when I lived every woman's fantasy: I killed my family. It was an unforgettable show about music and murder.

Tom and I in 1990, eating our way through Europe on our honeymoon. I weighed 240 pounds. Tom weighed 320 pounds. This was just before we started our diets.

*Arnie (Tom Arnold) and Nancy's (Sandra Bernhard)
wedding in Vegas with me, Jenny, and Jake as witnesses.*

Tom and I during the Halloween show in 1991.

Christmas 1992, celebrating with (l–r) Laurie Metcalf, Estelle Parsons, and Shelley Winters—the "Harris" women.

Here I am at an AIDS benefit in Utah, headed by my brother Ben, sporting the "beehive" state hairdo.

Dishing talk and food with Joan Collins.

*(l–r) Jessica, Brandi, Tom, Jake, Roseanne, and Jenny at
Jake's Bar Mitzvah in 1993. L' Shana tovah!*

"I have proof," Bill insisted over the ph
proof that your friend Mister Tom Arnold
tabloids about you."

"What kind of proof other than ninety p

"Ha-ha, Roseanne. How can you let this gu
you? How can you trust him? Look, he's been
checks from the *National Enquirer*. I saw then
heard this before, that Tom had been receiving
from the *Enquirer*. When I asked him about it, Tom
tered something about "typical bullshit," and, with so
apprehension, I sort of let it pass, in my way of letti
things pass and getting run over in the passing.

"So what's this proof you have, Bill?"

"I have a tape of him talking to different *Enquirer*
and *Star* reporters. I'm almost embarrassed to play it,
frankly."

"Uh-huh. And how'd you get the tape?"

"I hired a private eye." Naturally. Everyone had a
snitch, a private eye, a beard, a contact, a reporter. Everyone was wired (Tom, especially, but on cocaine, not
transmitters; also at this point, Tom was bending to the
pressure, getting crushed), everyone had a secret and because knowledge is power, everyone was walking around
with gleaming pecs and tight butts. And it broke my
heart to hear about the tape. Bill claimed there was stuff
on the tape where Tom even made some crude remarks
about my body. Bingo—hit her where she lives!!

I called Tom and he denied everything, but at that time, I felt hurt and betrayed—nothing new, really—and I had Tom immediately fired from the show. In a world devoid of trust, and even in the good old days, I trusted no one, including Tom. I learned a little something about it spending most of my life waiting for somebody to do me in the eye. It took me all of two hours to regret it and then another two hours to fight off principle and call the son of a bitch.

"Hi."

"Rosey?"

"Yeah. Uh . . . what're you doing?"

"What'd'you mean, what am I doing? I'm laying here—PRETTY SHOCKED . . ."

"Well . . . I want to ask you something. Even though you got fired and everything . . . do you think it would be okay if we still talked every night?"

"Fuuuuck you," he couched the words in a little, unhappy laugh—Tom knew how to fight, but he wasn't that good—and then hung up.

"Didn't think so," I said to the dial tone and hung up myself. The following day, Bill, that pot o' gold at the end of the *nolo contendere* rainbow, couldn't produce the tape. I waited one more day and he still had nothing to show for all of his bravado. Ninety proof.

I made Jeff offer Tom his job back the following day. Tom held out for a written contract this time. Smart guy. Still not accepted in the club, Tom did most of his

"Tommy" and "Cindy" at our July 3rd (1993) Bash.

writing at home. He finished the first draft of his work-story, "Guilt by Disassociation," and turned it in. Every-one agreed it was a quality script, but the other writers couldn't wait to get their grubby little fingers on it. The way the process is supposed to work is everyone makes notes, then turns them over to the original writer. In Tom's case, they blew off the notes and just plain rewrote his script. I wound up reading both versions, after the fact, and the rewrite was the worst script I've ever seen. They took all the guts out and jokes, it was just bullshit. And of course, I end up getting the job—gotta have that happy, Jiffy Pop ending, right? The only reason I got to see Tom's original script was because he had the balls to break "protocol" and bring it to me directly. When we neared production, I just threw out the writers' rewrite and shot all of Tom's script with the exception of one tiny "party" scene.

Now the other writers were absolutely furious with what Tom had done. They accused him of breaking the so-called code of ethics of writers and actors, and how they're supposed to be separate—never mind that he was *my* fiancée. Never mind that it was *my show.*

By late August, everybody hated Tom. He'd get into big arguments with Danny Jacobson in front of the other writers, the kind of fights that ended with people having to get between them to separate them. There was just so much negative energy there, you could feel your facial muscles tightening up before you entered the writers' building. Now they let Tom in the room with them—they were ordered to do so, or else—but made him feel as welcome as a garden snake and twice as low. Still, he managed to come up with good ideas. I wanted Tom to appear on my show—knowing my fans would tune in by the droves to see him. So we invented Arnie, who was supposed to be Dan's new sidekick. The writers, devoting their time to devising schemes which could lead to Tom's eventual dismissal instead of coming up with decent material for the show, gave us nothing but grief. In rehearsals, everyone gave Tom a hard time and the general consensus was that he couldn't cut it. We filmed on Friday, with a dress rehearsal the day before, Thursday. The director and producer called me aside to tell me that I looked like a fool bringing on my boyfriend. Tom was sick that week, and really nervous, so much so he thought about quitting the whole mess altogether.

Everyone was there for the dress rehearsal; the writers looked like they were mentally measuring Tom for a coffin. When it came time, though, Tom completely nailed it. The producers were happy and got even happier when the ratings came out. The show with Tom on it became the highest-rated "Roseanne" to date—44 share.

THE THOMAS CROWNSKI AFFAIR

"You gotta file for divorce, or this is it," Tom said. I promised him I would, on such and such a date, and he'd keep extending the deadline. He finally gave me one more day. Truth is I was scared to file, that leathery old fear of Bill running off with my kids the minute he hears about it flogging my backside. I pictured him hustling them into the car and driving off somewhere—he'd threatened to do so before—and I'd never see them again. Bill knew I had a soft spot about losing my kids, especially after having to give up Brandi.

"He ain't ever gonna do anything with your kids," Tom predicted, as though he had seen the future and for anyone messing with my kids, it was ugly, ugly, ugly. (Tom's knuckles were white, his jaw wiggled. He was scary.) I promised Tom I'd file again and once again chickened out. That's when Tom gave me an ultimatum: "Well, damnit, Rosey! You got till Friday."

I decided I was gonna have to step off the edge and had Tom drive me down to file. I came out howling and we celebrated, then got engaged on July 13. The night I filed for divorce, Tom and I decided to celebrate and have dinner at Spago. We'd never been there before. I'd rather eat at Big Boy myself, but Tom, being Mister Sociable, really wanted to go.

"This is a big deal—and now we can be seen in public," Tom insisted. "I think we should go someplace classy. You deserve it." What we didn't know was that as soon as you make a reservation at Spago, the press seems to get wind of it. By the time we got to the restaurant in West Hollywood, the place was crawling with photographers. They surrounded our car and wouldn't let us move. If we wanted to drive, we couldn't have; the flashes from the hundreds of pictures they took literally blinded us. Finally, we had to negotiate our way out with them, which made matters worse. Everyone knows you can't negotiate with terrorists. We told them they could all take one more picture if they would just let us pass. All that did was give them license to behave like chimpanzees.

Now they were leaping on my car, denting it to all hell, pressing their gruesome, sorry faces against the windshield, and I was getting claustrophobic. And hot, since the air conditioner doesn't work if you're sitting still. I had to roll the window down to get some air and that caused an even bigger commotion. People started running out of Tower Records (which is across the street from Spago). They thought it was Michael Jackson or somebody like that. After getting over the initial disappointment of discovering it was me, the crowd had this collective rally of the spirit (i.e., if you can't worship the star you worship, worship the one you're with) and decided to go with the flow. "Roseanne, Roseanne!" they began chanting, and now I had to sign autographs— while the photographers continued to mob my car.

Three big twenty-year-old boys, Midwestern types, wearing metal-head T-shirts came up to the car. Amused by our plight, they offered to "move them out" for fifty bucks. Well, we paid 'em, which was probably a big mistake since before you could say "duck sausage pizza" there was a huge rumble between the bunch of photographers and these three kids. We thought it had been pretty silly and ridiculous—the photographers, however, didn't.

The next day lawyers started calling. The week after that, the *National Enquirer* ran a story with my picture on the front page and the headline read, ROSEANNE GOES NUTS!

They got the perfect picture, too (they had enough to choose from). I've got this huge, all-American smile on my face, and on Tom's side of the car it's all sneers and fists and people beating each other up. Another picture showed me actually paying the kids money. That case is still pending since the photographers won't settle. We eventually had to settle for $20,000. No one was physically hurt, although one of the women photographers claims that she became psychotic as a result of the incident and is therefore unable to work.

The next elegant marriage ritual for Tom and me was the holy exchange of the tattoos. We always talked about them, thought it was funny and stupid—like us dressing up as twins, which we had been doing a lot of anyway, speaking of stupid. We got tattoos on our butts in Utah. As I was getting branded, Tom says, "I gotta tell you something, honey. Now that we've been tattooed and all, I mean it's closer than bein' married, isn't it? Remember back when you asked me about the *Enquirer*? Well, I cashed some of their checks."

"You what?" The vibration of the tattoo machine still hadn't worn off on my cheeks.

"I did get some money, I did cash the checks. I paid rent with them and bought drugs with them, honey." Tom ticked off each offense, his fingers fluttering inces-

santly the way they always do when he talks and
schemes. "We had this plan together, remember? Whatever it took, right?" He went on. Part of this was true.
He needed money 'cause I routinely stiffed him for the
jokes he wrote. Sure, I was mad but I also had his goddamn name etched on my butt, which meant I had little
chance of working up a good head on my anger. You
know that great scene in *The Thomas Crown Affair*
where Faye Dunaway and Steve McQueen are finally real
truthful with each other in this great steam room in a
townhouse in Boston? And they're all sweaty and gor-
geous and wrapped in these luxurious towels? Well, it
was nothing like that.

"You told me to do whatever it took, remember?
Look, the checks came in the mail, made out to me, and
I cashed them to pay my rent."

After I thought about it for a while, I cooled down.
Hell, I would've cashed the checks, too, probably. And
from the *Enquirer*, I'd still do it, even today.

The print media? They're all sculptors and demoli-
tions experts. They think they create you (in their eyes) in
order to bring you down when the next buildable thing
comes along. To them, I'm the fat housewife who stum-
bled out of her trailer and accidentally said something
funny once or twice. They'll come and interview me, ask
me all this profound shit, and I answer with some measure of respect and intelligence. Then at the end, they'll

throw in the most bullshit question they can think of and out of a two-hour interview, that's the part they'll print. I don't know why they ask for two hours of my time. Why not just ask for five minutes and go, "How much do you weigh?" I weigh a hundred and eighty pounds. "All right, thank you. The rest we'll get from old back issues of the *Enquirer*." I mean, why do they waste my time? And they all say the same thing when they're leaving my house. "Man—you are so *intelligent*. And nobody knows it." Yeah, because they censor any sign of intelligence out of the articles.

"Well, that's not gonna happen here," the guy from *Playboy* promised. Sure. Then the interview comes out and it's "The fat, jolly Roseanne would love to eat her fudge brownies and wrestle with her husband, another fat person. By the way, Tom sold stories to the *Enquirer* and they're both known to have tattoos on their asses. They fuck a lot, eat too much, and have a farm."

Here's something I learned about the press from watching Frank Sinatra. Every fourth story about you should be really negative and the three in between should be positive. If you studied Frank's press clippings you'd see first that he'd buy a car for somebody, a homeless person, then you'd see that he had a hospital opened for children, and after that there'd be something about giving money to cure some disease. Finally, you'd read that he had supposedly done something unspeakable.

And you know what? The *Enquirer* is the most powerful piece of literature in this country. And you know what else? Once you're in good with them, they're the most trustworthy people in the world. But first you have to win a lawsuit against them.

BENEDICT CANYON

alf of me wanted Tom to give up his apartment and move in with me; the other half wanted him to stay where he was, fearing that seeing all two hundred fifty pounds of him every day, full-strength among the toothpaste and the coffee cake, the bloom might fall off the Rosey. The half that feared an allergic reaction to any kind of live-in arrangement manifested itself in many vexing mutations that probably drove Tom crazy. Early on, he begged me not to have him move in.

"I gotta keep my apartment. I *gotta* keep my apartment," he kept moaning. He should've just come out and said he needed it to entertain the Laker girls and the Dodger usherettes and to have Roman eat-and-puke parties with his friends because that's what I was thinking when he kept insisting on keeping it.

"I just know where everything is there. I'm attached to my bathroom. I like my bathroom, Rosey—"

"No, no—you gotta get out of there. You have to move in," I hounded him. He finally gave in.

The day came for Tom to move in. He made at least eighteen trips back and forth from his apartment to my house in Benedict Canyon, in a car that died on every hill, on a day that was hot enough to fry your eyeballs. My anxiety level had a logarithmic relationship to the amount of different furniture hauled through the doors; the more I saw, the more I had the urge to fly out of the house and look for someone I could catch yellow fever from, just to have a decent excuse for Tom to get all this strange shit out of my sight, strange shit that meant a foreign presence, an alien life form that told jokes, took shit from absolutely no one, snorted coke (though at the time, I was still sold on the allergy story), and could eat his way into the *Guinness Book of Records.* He was sweating, his knuckles bleeding, with chunks of skin hanging from them, battered from the all-day move when he set down his television set, the last of his possessions, when I finally worked up the courage to tell him that I'd changed my mind.

"Aw . . . I don't think you should move in, uh, Tom—it's just not gonna work."

"Well, I'm all for things that work. Say, does this room have three-prong outlets?"

"I'm not kidding, Tom."

"You're not kidding. Well, that just about describes our whole relationship, doesn't it? You making a decision, you changing your mind, and after about fifty of those, me just doing what I gotta do."

"I'm sorry. I just changed my mind, Tom. I just can't go through with it. Will you forgive me?" Tom looked at his skinned knuckles for a spell, then this look of overwhelming agony gathered at the bridge of his nose, as though someone had flossed his sinuses with a toilet chain.

"Rosey, I'm . . . I'm gonna stay here for, say, one week, okay?"

"Okay, but why one week?"

"Because I'm tired, honey. I'm tired from moving and hurting myself moving and it's gonna take me that long to get my strength back in order to hit you as hard as I need to hit you."

The children decided to make Tom feel at home, had home been a marine barracks under investigation for criminal hazing. The first thing they did was steal all of his sweat socks—he had over seventy pairs, an idiosyncrasy that might've gone back to his meat-packing days. He found his best pair of shoes out in the driveway, under the wheels of a car, and they stole money from his wallet daily. He took Jess to the market one day and noticed she had eighty dollars in her purse.

"Wow—how'd you make all that, Jess?" Tom innocently asked her.

"Well, I, uh . . . borrowed it from you."

"*Did* you? I don't remember that."

"Oh . . . okay. I took it without telling you that I borrowed it."

"Have you done that before?"

"Yeah," she replied, with a benign, almost shy smile. She had a way of giving you the shaft and making you feel good about it—definitely not a character trait she got from Bill's side of the family.

"Okay, well, I'll tell you what. Just don't tell me when you do it because I'd rather not have to deal with it each time."

"Sure, Tom. I can do that for you."

"Great, great. This is good, this is progress here. Um, just one other thing though. What you're doing with the money? It isn't borrowing, okay?"

"Okay," Jessica cooed, as if they'd just both made this real estate deal and she'd agreed to come down a couple grand on the price. She had elevated the art of lying to a science—now that she got from the Clan of the Cave Bill.

Jennifer is a master locksmith. And she has been since she was twelve. She can pick locks, take them apart—tumblers, springs, rods, all that stuff that I have trouble holding, let alone working with—and completely rebuild them. She wanted locks on her doors for "privacy," which is to say "no good." When we learned that she was smoking in there, we called the locksmith to have the locks removed. The locksmith came in the morning, used a special tool to completely dismantle the lock, and put the parts—there had to be a couple dozen near-microscopic pieces—in a plastic bag. We needed the lock for when we would eventually move, and Tom put it down in the basement. By the evening, when Tom got back from work, Jenny had completely rebuilt the lock, performed all these intricate assemblies and adjustments without tools. We think she used a bobby pin and a butter knife—that, or black magic. When the locksmith came back to take the lock off again he was astonished. "There's no way she could've done this," he marveled. She did it. Trust me.

When they got bored with creating havoc with Tom's life, my children belovedly turned to their mother. My wardrobe was constantly being plundered, and occasionally for something to wear even, which was nice because there was a remote chance of getting the item back. Most of the time, however, it was for the sheer sport of it, like a pack of stray dogs ravaging a Dumpster for the hell of it. I found one of my expensive leather belts cut up in pieces in Jess's drawer. Her alibi was that she found it in her drawer, that the maid must've put it there, and *that's* why she cut it up—she thought it was hers.

Jess got a spy kit for her birthday. Now she could eavesdrop with the best of the Nixon White House Gang. Her nanny, a really sweet woman, could never have a boyfriend because Jenny always listened in on all her phone calls—she could hear Jenny eating and breathing on the other line. She did it to us, too, and eventually found a way to listen in on just about every call that came into that house. When you gotta run down to the liquor store to make a private phone call because your kids have tapped all the phones and then you have trouble getting back in because they've messed with the locks, well, let's just say you're at a place in that great bell curve of normal family structure where there isn't a whole helluva lot of headroom.

I was always protective of my kids; I wanted to nurture their creativity, to help them soar, never to allow them the inhibitions that barged into my childhood and turned it ugly.

I raised my daughters to be Witches. I did, and they are. They're very powerful but now they have to get some of the earth in them. They don't have any earth in them. I used to let them wear big hats and big boa feathers when they were little, riding their bikes and Big-Wheels all over the neighborhood. I wanted them to have very few restrictions. My daughters, consequently, have grown up to be incredible women.

Jenny, my middle daughter, is a mathematical prodigy. She took a Barbie doll and calculated what her measurements would be like if she were a real human being. Barbie would be six feet, two inches. Her hands and her feet would be four inches long. Her neck would be six inches long. Her waist would be seventeen inches and her bust would be thirty-four inches or twice as big as her waist. Her torso would be thirteen inches while her legs would measure forty-five inches.

Both of my daughters are into myths and whatnot—I suppose they could meet some freaky beatniks someday. I used to love to play Barbie dolls with them. I still love to play Barbie dolls by myself. I love to dress them, comb their hair, make their plans for the day. But the whole unconventional lifestyle I created for them has its downside. We were in therapy once when one of my daughters remarked, "Mom, you made us think that the only people we could like were black, Jewish lesbians."

I got from point A (a roiling nightmare of Dickensian struggle) to point B (power, self-expression, economic, and to a certain point, spiritual freedom) and lived to tell the tale. It all comes down to Maya Angelou, i.e., "I know why the caged bird sings." I hate to feed into that whole artist-must-suffer thing because we know what that creates: explorers, Lewis and Clarks looking for fun and trouble—hothouse suffering, freeze-dried decay and excuses. But I guess it's true. You take all your pain and suffering and turn it into a really beautiful song. The addictive part and the creative part of us are side by side. That's why they're often together. What I was hoping for my kids, however, was a chance to get from point A to point B by taking the "A" train, nonstop, no excess baggage.

These are the things I wanted my children to know, to understand, to appreciate. I thought I was the fertilizer and they were the victory garden, but in the end, I wound up with vegetables the size of something gone amuck in a Japanese sci-fi movie. The nurturing hippie baloney only meant no limits, no discipline, no boundaries, no nothing. I wanted to be their friend—I didn't know how to be a parent, since my own were space people.

By the time we moved into the Benedict Canyon house, the kids were full-blown lunatics, wild, crazy, sneaking out, going to the midnight showing of *The Rocky Horror Picture Show*, smoking, putting their cigarettes out in the rugs, dyeing their hair black, spilling the hair dye into the carpet, wearing black nails, black clothes, black eye makeup, and just celebrating life in general by hating all the success and especially the child-of-a-celebrity shit.

"God, we were all so happy in Denver" was a common complaint. What made everything so great there? Getting their clothes at Goodwill? Eating macaroni every night in a place where no one liked you 'cause you were the only Jews? Is that what was so fucking happy about

the place? Or was it because Bill and I, as the quintessen-
tial Ma 'n' Pa, were so gawddamned HAPPY?

I think what was so scary for them was not that I
became famous, but because (when it happened) it happened so quickly. I was Mom, just Mom, who everybody
takes a swing at, Mom the big house cat, always good for
a laugh and a coupla bucks, not to mention being the
best eat-to-commiserate pal who ever cried through a funeral, a screwed-up boyfriend, or a betraying girlfriend
while boring through a kitchen table full of deviled eggs
and little sandwiches. One minute she's just Mom, someone to fight over the hot rollers with, and the next thing
you know she's famous and everybody likes her. And
then this guy who really loves her moves in—and he
won't cut you any slack to save his sorry, four-lane ass.

Jenny had this habit of lying outside my bedroom
door and screaming at the top of her lungs if the door
was locked and, heaven forbid, I might require some privacy. She could've knocked, but then again, if she
would've, she wouldn't have been my daughter. Anyway,
I was used to it, but Tom, who had a passing acquain-
tance with more conventional means of announcing your
presence, was not. When Jenny tried it, Tom went out,
picked her up, carried her to her room, and closed the
door, which didn't sit particularly well with Jenny. She
ran through the house, screaming, "HE BEAT ME UP!
HE BEAT ME UP!"

Jenny didn't like the fact that Tom, with arms like a

front loader, could physically move her. That was part of her act. Glower and be big. So big that no one could move her.

Jess's act was just to be a huge manipulator and lie all the time and I believed anything she said. Tom knew a few things about lying (since he'd been hiding a titanic drug addiction from me at the time) and he was on to Jess's scam like a bloodhound. We'd cheerfully accept her story on doing this or that, then Tom would follow her and find out she'd be doing just the opposite. Being an information dirt-devil, Tom would read their diaries—hey, the rules were being broken left and right; when kids don't play by the rules, then you can't, either, if you're gonna save them from the entire new food groupings of vices and dangers. It was intervention, big-time, but it saved their lives, too.

I started reading their diaries, too. They'd leave them unlocked for me with a little note inside that said, "Mom—the good stuff's on page forty-five." I think they started writing this brilliant but obvious fiction after a while just to shock me. I considered this a definite sign of improvement, since they used to hit me, bite me, scratch me, and pinch me before Tom came along. Along the way, I somehow taught them not to respect anybody, and they didn't—most of all, me.

It was Tom, the biggest anarchist ever to piss on a cop's shoes, who really started laying the laws down with the children.

"First thing," he told them, "is you don't use abusive language with your mother or tell her to shut up, get bent, go fuck herself—ax that stuff right now." They never heard anything like that before and it hit 'em like that stun gun they used on Rodney King—only he went down.

"WHAT? Who the hell are you?" one of them bellowed. My kids could bellow real good, too.

"You're a fascist—that's what you are," Jenny sneered at Tom, her former bigness now dwarfed when he stood up—a Frigidaire towering over a picnic cooler.

"No, you don't talk to your mother like that," Tom blithely persisted. "And you know what, you do things for your mother." And they *never* heard that 'cause Bill, all he ever did was blame me for everything, i.e., "Mom left us all for her little job"—not that I was paying the bills and working. Another one of Bill's vintage lines, after complaining about me working got a little shopworn when I made a ton of money and he sat home figuring out how to spend it, was "You know, Tom doesn't really love your mom. He just wants her money." So they resented me, and used my body as a punching bag or a scratching post. When Tom came along, he put an end to that, too. I had one daughter lunge at my throat while we were on an airplane; she was upset because I wouldn't let her smoke. Tom guided her back down into her seat.

"You don't touch her. That's your mother. You don't

touch her. You're all going to be . . . lovely women. Understand?"

Before they understood, or became lovely, we had more groundings than a month of fog over Heathrow airport.

"I wanna go sit in the car with one of my friends," Jess begged Tom. She was serving time for her latest infraction and confined to the yard. "I swear to God I won't leave," she promised, and because we were more lenient then—we had erroneously used leniency as an antidote to guilt, which made us feel a little better, but kicked the hell out of the kids' perspective—we let her. Tom went to check on her an hour later, she was gone. When she returned a few hours later, Tom was waiting for her at the gate.

"That's it. Now you're grounded for the month," Tom said. She climbed out of a car laden with bald guys and guys with Mohawks, guys who looked blissfully dazed and confused, like some very pissed-off farmer let 'em have it between the eyes with a fence post.

"Oh, man," she cried. "You embarrassed me in front of my friends."

At night, the girls used to run up an astronomical phone bill calling up those 900 talk lines, you know, the kind the TV commercials show with these teenagers just having the time of their lives with a phone plugged in their ear, and AIDS, gang wars, teenage pregnancy, and budget cuts causing eight of them to share a math book are some other bozo's problems. The girls do excellent hair whips and play with the phone cord like it was some guy's pecker. And the guy in the commercial who's supposed to be on the other end of the line and looks like the offspring of Troy Donahue and Sandra Dee reacts like he's been blown out of his shoes over the outrageous thing he's just heard. Only this time it was Tom who heard it. He got up to go to the bathroom one night around midnight and heard talking upstairs—the girls were on the phone.

"Hey, girls, hang up the phone, it's past twelve and you got school tomorrow," Tom told them from the extension downstairs. Sure, sure, they said. At one, they were still talking. By three in the morning, after they had routinely ignored his second request, Tom picked up the phone, ready with all kinds of lethal and unpleasant threats, when he decided to listen in for a minute.

"You know, do, uh, you take a shower every day," a male voice was asking, "because I'll tell ya, my last girlfriend didn't and she smelled really bad." After the girls assured the sleazeball that they indeed showered daily, he got downright philosophical. "You know, I feel like I'm friends with you guys, and I feel friends should be able to have sex."

"I been sayin' that since junior high," Jenny (in junior high) agreed, and that's when Tom cut in:

"HEY! THESE GIRLS ARE TWELVE AND

THIRTEEN YEARS OLD, YOU WEIRDO! I'M GONNA FIND OUT YOUR NAME AND KICK YOUR ASS!"

"WE ARE NOT THIRTEEN! YOU LIAR!"

The girls refused to talk to Tom the next day.

On another occasion, however, Tom and I did humiliate Jess in the name of parental imperative. We were both suspicious of her boyfriend, whom we hadn't met in person yet, and Tom was angling for a way to get him to the house. So he called him at his home.

"Listen, buddy, we're having a surprise wet T-shirt contest for Jess's birthday—lotta kids are gonna be over and, uh, we'd love to have ya over!" Jess wasn't as thrilled with the ploy as we were. We apologized profusely, took responsibility for humiliating her, then put away clothing we didn't want cut up, just in case.

I guess at first the kids were a little afraid of Tom Unchained and all. But they always seemed to wind up coming to him, rallying around him. When a girlfriend of Jess's sold information about her to the *National Enquirer*, Tom offered to go to school with Jess as moral support the day she decided to confront her. The girl's father happened to be at the school that day, too. Tom and the father got into a shouting match, Tom threatening to break the man's (fucking) fingers when he stuck them in Tom's chest. Then Jess and her girlfriend started pushing each other around. Now that's togetherness. White trash "Family Feud." Hey, class is for the schmucks who take life as a spectator sport anyway, so who needs it? Not our happy family, no way. Gimme pink and lime green, a splatter pattern in the Formica, fat neckties, an honest belch, and a one-note cheek samba any day. And you can stick that goddamned shellfish fork you-know-where, okay?

The kids loved Tom for his gentle side and in the most important regard, reading their diaries notwithstanding, he was forthright with them: "You know, I really love your mom. And I can be your friend or I can be your stepfather, and I need to be your stepfather right now." They could never hate him after that. And, having a stepmother of his own, he understood some of what they were experiencing at the time, he knew where the resentment came from, how the mistrust and contempt muscled their way to the front of every confrontation. He knew how they suffered. And it probably kept him from killin' 'em a couple of times over. Lovely women. Or, at least they are now.

My son, Jake, was eleven years old when Tom moved in. The extent of Jake's dad-like paranoia manifested itself one day when Tom and he were playing tennis out in our front yard. Tom was his usual self, swearing, screaming, hollering when he missed a shot.

"Be quiet," Jake said. "Somebody'll come and shoot us."

"What? Nobody's gonna shoot us. Where'd you get a fool idea like that?" Tom scoffed. Ya think maybe from

Bill, who always talked that way and always kept guns around the house and made sure that we knew he had guns? "Let them try to shoot us, Jake, I'll kick their fucking ass." Jake liked that.

All of the kids, Tom, and myself, have grown up together, grown closer and healthier during the last five years.

LET'S TAKE A
MEETING

In an act that belongs up there with that South Korean minister who pronounced the end of the world coming sometime early in 1991—no, an act that ranks up there with the thousands of dumb-shits who sold all their worldly possessions and gave their *money to this minister*—Jeff Harris decided to fire Tom. Danny Jacobson went to Jeff and gave him one of those him-or-me choices and to Jeff it was like choosing between Häagen-Dazs and a scoop of shit. Oh, and Tom and I were engaged at the time. Like I said, ignorance and arrogance hand-in-hand. . . . It was so cool because once I had Tom Arnold, it was all fucking over. But first, he had to be fired.

"I don't think I quite get what you're saying," Tom tried to sort things out, to make sense of what he was hearing in Jeff's office that day when he called him in. Jeff tried to be gracious; it came off as condescending instead.

"Well, we think you're a really big talent, but, uh . . . it just might not work out."

"How so?" Tom asked. Jeff was smoking a cigar at the time, blowing on the ash lightly, to make it glow.

"To tell you the truth, a lot of the other writers are jealous of the time you seem to spend with Roseanne. You showed up at John Goodman's wedding with her and . . . well . . ."

"Well . . . we're engaged. Look, Jeff, what are you trying to say here?" Jeff shrugged with a kind of dramatic self-consciousness that usually dissembles a sense of self-perceived cleverness.

"I'm saying cease and desist, I guess. Yeah."

" 'Cease and desist'? 'Cease and desist'? What the hell is that? What're you, some kind of probation officer? What're you saying? I'm not supposed to see Rosey?"

"No—no, not that. That's not what I'm saying." Jeff was getting frustrated. "Look, I don't want you working here anymore. I'll pay ya—don't worry about it, you'll be paid for the rest of the season. I guess what I'm saying is clean out your desk. You're fired."

Tom, as big as a lighthouse, slowly got up, stood there for a minute, towering over Jeff. Then he promptly uncoiled, unwound like a reel with a goddamn marlin on its hook. He grabbed Jeff by his collar, and threw him on the couch like a sack of compost.

"I'M NOT FIRED! YOU'RE FIRED, FUCKER!" Tom was shaking and choking Jeff, who, by the way, suffered from a dystrophic leg. "I'M NOT FIRED, JEFF! YOU'RE FIRED! And let me tell you something else"— Tom finally let him go—"You're lucky I don't beat up cripples!"

Then Tom came looking for me.

"Hey," he said. "This guy Jeff Harris just tried to fire me." And then I said something, something completely out of character, something all those fat-assed hacks would've creamed in their Dockers to hear.

"Well," I murmured, "he is the boss." I suppose this moment, under the pyrotechnics and the posturing, the arrogance hanging in the air, lingering and static like scorching weather that won't go away, I suppose this was my Gethsemane, my moment of doubt where I began to nod off, like some one-eyed giant, dopey from wine, who'd finally had enough.

I needed someone to be with me to tell me what was real because I couldn't tell myself. I missed everything but the decay. I couldn't see the light. Maybe I could see it at one point in time, but as a child my parents accidentally and unknowingly took a stick and gouged my eye socket away from the corners of my eyes and turned them inward. Now I am only able to see my fishy brain impulses and nothing else.

And that's when Tom, vital and coping, slugging it out with whoever was out to take his boots from him before he was dead, fighting the good fight against improvident talking heads and his own internal car crashes, saved me. I saw myself being dragged by the Television City chariot. Tom put it all in perspective.

"What? He's the boss? HE'S THE BOSS? Bullshit! *You're* the boss," Tom was hollering in that way of his that makes you think the hurricane El Niño is coming up through the soles of his shoes. "You go straight up to that powwow writers' room where they can't buy a good idea, and raise some real hell. You tell them, 'Each of you ought to be kissing my ass for me *allowing* you to write on my show. 'Cause none of you have any goddamn talent. And, number two: Don't come to me anymore to disagree. Don't come to me with that "everyone thinks we should" shit because you know what? This is not a fucking democracy. It's a Queendom.' "

So I did. They all looked at me like I took charm and poise lessons from Lizzie Borden, like I channeled Joe Stalin into the room.

After that, Jeff took an ad out in *Variety* that said

something like AFTER THIS SEASON OF ROSEANNE, I'M GOING TO THE RELATIVE PEACE AND QUIET OF BEIRUT. Yeah, well they ain't gonna think you're funny there, either.

Jeff got to stay on until the end of the season, sort of as a lame duck—sorry, poor choice of words—and he spent the rest of his time entertaining old-boy-type friends in his office.

Tom has the hugest balls in the world. Someone once described him as being "someone who doesn't care and what's really bad is he doesn't care that he doesn't care." On the last day of the season, Jeff and his buddies were in Jeff's office, gathered round the piano, drinking Scotch and singing Neil Simon songs. Christ, I can't take Simon and his "I'm locked out here in the hall in nothing but my undershorts. Lemme in!! Unlock the goddamn door, Gloria!!" starring Walter Matthau. Tom breezed into Jeff's office, unannounced, with a video camera on his shoulder. Jeff had friends in there with him and Tom aimed the camera on all of them.

"So, Jeff—say good-bye, buddy. But first, tell me what furniture you're taking to BEIRUT with you because this is gonna be my fucking office next year." All of Jeff's friends cracked up until Jeff glared at them and they became quiet again.

After the failed coup to fire Tom, Tom and I went to Carsey-Werner to get control of the show. What made this a watershed event for me was the fact that we did it without Arlyne, my manager, who'd always functioned as my go-between with these people. Yeah, well, the days of refraction, of seeing things through the bent eyes of someone else, were over. No more beards or mouth-pieces. Word of our plan got around quicker than hell would scorch a feather (information in Hollywood beats out the speed of light in a drag race; information has its own special relativity). The night before we went to the network, we got a call from Jeff Harris. He was pleading, "Please let me work on the show. I'll do anything, I'll change it, I'll make Tom producer—I'll do anything."

The next day we had our meeting with Carsey-Werner. Jeff, who attended the meeting, had his balls back, talking tough. Tom Werner and Marcy Carsey would make a point and Jeff would add little things like "That's right . . . we're running the show this way, and . . ." Blah blah blah.

"Would you shut up?" Tom railed, and finally Carsey-Werner asked Jeff to leave.

Our next stop was Bob Iger's Presidential office at ABC—another first for us, since, again, we were navigating without Arlyne at the tiller, but also we were going over Carsey-Werner's head. Doing an end around on Carsey-Werner probably wouldn't have been necessary had we known what our relationship was with them at the time, but it was another case of fear and misinforma-tion coming from both sides. In actuality, we had—

have—a good relationship with Carsey-Werner. They don't interfere, they trust us, and they advise with scrutiny and tact. But at the time, to us, Carsey and Werner were scary people. "Don't trust them, they're assholes. Don't trust them and don't talk to them," Arlyne cautioned us. We'd hear horror stories from her—most of them fiction—her motive not protection but only to galvanize her hold over me, as she suggested we get rid of them and then make her an executive producer.

Tom's nose bled most of the day when we met with Bob Iger.

"My allergies are acting up," he told me and all I could think was he must be allergic to everything on the planet. I didn't know it at the time, but he went into Bob Iger's office completely coked up. At one point during the meeting Tom even excused himself, went into the ABC bathroom, and snorted up some more coke, just to make it through the remainder of the meeting. But as ripped as Tom was, he still managed to deconstruct all the bullshit out of what was, in all respects, a pretty profound moment.

"Look, uh, there's not a whole helluva lot I can do above and beyond what Tom and Marcy had to offer." Bob Iger shrugged.

"Well, wait a minute," Tom put up his hands. "I used to work at Hormel and I'll tell you what—"

"The *meat* people?"

"Yeah. And there was a boss. That was the head guy, the guy that made all the decisions on everybody. And that would be you, the way I look at it."

"Okay . . ." Bob Iger nodded patiently.

"And if a supervisor of a department—let's say that department was the "Roseanne" show—disagreed with the head boss on something, it seemed like the head guy would get the final decision. I mean, that's the way we worked it there." Bob Iger seemed to extract something from Tom's little analogy.

"Yeah . . . well . . . yeah," he agreed.

"See, at the meat-packing plant, we did things a little different. I expected the network to be run at least that efficiently."

After Tom got Jeff fired and we took over as executive producers, things lightened up and got better. Bob Iger received a big promotion and told me, face-to-face, "I want you to know that *I* know I got this promotion because of the improved atmosphere at your show. And I owe you one."

How nice of ABC to repay me by canceling my first and second projects at his network, including "The Jackie Thomas Show" (canceled instead of moved to another night, as NBC did with "Seinfeld" the following season), which finished its run ten points higher in the ratings than "Seinfeld" that same year. "Jackie Thomas" was ABC's fifth highest rated show and finished seventh in demographics for *all* television. ABC renewed "Dinosaurs" though, and signed big deals with Oliver Stone and David Lynch—neither of whom broke the top thirty with their shows.

"Jackie Thomas" was far ahead of its time and I'm proud of it. Boy, at least the workers at Hormel have a union.

DOUBLE LIVES

T om and I were asked to honor Bette Midler at her birthday party. I had one glass of wine and something snapped. Maybe all the alcohol from that particular bottle wound up in that glass or maybe someone slipped a hit of acid or some chloral hydrate into it. Whatever it was, I turned into a runaway eighteen-wheeler and all I could do was lay on the air horn. First person I flattened was Brandon Tartikoff, who was then head of NBC.

"Brandon"—I leaned over into his space—"now,

why don't you give me a job? Because I hate ABC. I hate them fuckers and I don't want to be on that fucking network. You give me a show on your network."

"Okay, Roseanne," Brandon indulged me with a chuckle.

"I'm dead serious. I want to be on NBC." We all had a big laugh over it—me, Tom, and Brandon. Of course, I was kidding—at the time.

At work, at that time, laughs were a little harder to come by for Tom. With him as everybody's unanimous choice as the leper of the "Roseanne" show production offices, Tom's work environment wasn't what you would exactly call ideal. Now you dangle around a drug addict in a stressful environment and you're gonna wind up with some trouble. Tom didn't fall off the wagon—he did the long jump.

Me, my poison of choice was pot. I smoked it every day for years. Trust me, it's a narcotic. I tried everything—but everything just led back to pot. That was all I really liked. I was certain, at the time, that the pot was linked to my creativity. I was getting high, writing, getting high, writing.

For whatever reason—codependency, narcissism, matriarchy, or just for the god-blessed fun of it, I wanted Tom to smoke pot, like I was. Even after he had gone through a brief detox during that summer of '89 and was attending AA meetings, I'd try and get him to toke up with me, reasoning that pot was really harmless. Here's where I tripped up. Pot illuminated otherwise obscure perceptions, and silenced all the quibbling voices within me until there was only one. Stoned on pot, Tom wound up with only one voice, too. Only his told him to get more cocaine.

At that time, cocaine was really cheap in L.A., especially if you bought it in quantity. And Tom was the supply sergeant of quantity. I knew he was using; I just didn't know how much until much later, during rehab, when he opened up and confessed everything. Where I thought he was scoring in grams, Tom was buying by the quarter pound. And then he used as if the fate of the human race depended on him snorting up enough coke to scorch the inside of his skull, chopping and spreading out the white stuff with the gusto and speed of a Benihana chef. In those days, there wasn't a line around that he was too proud to bow for—he had seen the fine grain of coffee tables up close so many times he probably could've made a swell furniture refinisher.

I got a brief glimpse of the future as far back as my first HBO special, which he wrote and appeared in, playing my slothful, beer-swilling Barcalounger husband. In the final scene of my trailer skit, Tom and I are supposed to rediscover each other, as he approaches me with love-pious eyes. He tears himself away from a ball game he is watching on TV and takes me in his arms.

"But what about your game?" my line goes.

"It's halftime, honey," Tom answers in a sexy voice.

As he's gazing down into my eyes, I could see the insides of his nostrils. They were caked with cocaine—and it wasn't part of the script, either.

The thing about Tom is he was born without an off switch to begin with. As a hyperactive child, he suffered from attention deficit syndrome, a condition that was partially controlled through drug therapy. To keep little Tommy from hanging from the light fixtures and eating the blackboard chalk, he was given Ritalin, a drug that works as a stimulant in adults but in children has the effect of a sedative. As an adult substance abuser, Tom found a snoutful of cocaine actually to have a calming effect on him, making his attachment to blow all the more nefarious.

Leading two lives, Tom kept the wide scope of his addiction from me as long as he could, getting a primo assist from my own denial. He rarely left the house and when he did, it was to hook up with his drug dealer. He'd be in bed with me by eight every night, then after I'd fallen asleep, he'd roam through the house at all hours, creaking the floorboards and doing even more coke. By the time he'd worked his tolerance up to doing a half an ounce a day, it's safe to say the cocaine was no longer relaxing him. When I began to suspect that his drug usage was more than just pot-smoking he denied it, told me I was crazy. The more he did, the sloppier he got. I'd find coke crumbs on the floor, blood (he'd ruptured blood vessels in his nose) on the towels, closets where he'd hide to snort coke in disarray with coats and hangers all over the floor. He wouldn't sleep for five-day stretches, attributing it to insomnia caused by the oppressive atmosphere of the show. No longer able to maintain the charade at home, he started going out a lot more until even that became impossible. One Saturday, I got a call from one of the neighbors:

"Tom's parked down the hill. He can't get through the gate," she told me in a tone of voice that insinuated excessive behavior was afoot. I drove down to pick him up, found him sitting in his car, ashamed and already resentful, figuring in a few minutes, I'd be tearing into him again. He'd been out driving around on cocaine time, which meant each moment was a thousand times more or less profound than the previous one, depending on how close you were to crashing, and Tom was crashing real bad. He was so bad, he forgot the code for the electronic gate and had to flag down the neighbor. I expected him to hand me the usual ratty bouquet of wilted excuses. He just sat there, pathetic and beaten. The space where our dependable war usually took place was instead filled with the revelation that this man's life was no longer his own; and me, upping the bid with selfish threats and intimidation, wasn't gonna change a damn thing. Helping him out of the car, I gave him a hug and took him home.

Tom stayed in bed for the next twenty-four hours, while the sweat sloshed off him like a waterfall. I took his wallet to pay for some ice cream. Pulling out his credit card, I noticed there was powder on it. I licked it and it was cocaine. Full in my face.

I couldn't deny anymore, so I moved out. I beat it, I ran away, sent the kids to Bill's, and moved in with my assistant from the show. For the next two days Tom tried calling me but I refused to have any contact with him. That was it, we were finished as far as I was concerned. After he promised to tell me the truth if I came home, I went to see him at the house. He looked like death's kissin' cousin—pride, self-esteem, worthiness, these were keepsakes from a long, long time ago and now they flickered under the bonfire of misery in his eyes.

"I can't stop using, Rosey. I hate myself. I want so bad to tell you I'll stop but I can't. I can't stop and I'm scared shitless I'm going to die."

It wouldn't be the first time I heard this kind of talk, either. Some months before Tom and I began living together, he was using heavily, too. The day I got to meet my daughter, after eighteen years, I received a call from Tom's roommate.

"Tom is hemorrhaging through his nose and I'm afraid he's gonna die. I think you should come and get him to the hospital." I didn't understand addiction, yet. I thought he could stop. That night, after returning from the hospital where I checked Tom in, and taking Brandi and her mother back to their hotel, after dinner, I just sat in my Jeep in Westwood and cried until the sky turned black.

Tom and I were planning to be married on January 20 at the last event ever held at the world-famous Coconut Grove. Aside from the show, my kids, my husband-problems, I also found time to plan a wedding. I'd already spent a hundred thousand dollars on it, with the floors, walls, everything in black and white and red, and now it was all over. Tom was checked in at detox, in Century City—for the second time in less than a year. I wasn't about to marry a cokehead, expose my children to some lying, nosebleeding high-wire act. No way.

I leaked it to the news that our wedding was off—that's how Tom learned about it—while he was in detox watching TV. After he'd been in for a few days, my resentment subsided enough for me to go down there and confront him about all the lying he'd done to me. First thing he wanted to know about was the wedding.

"Hey, are we, you know, gonna get married, or, or what?" Tom could shuffle his feet without using them.

"You and your drug problem. You ruined everything, you dumb bastard." I know I was supposed to be hurt—and I was—but anger, as a tool, required no assembly or instruction manual. I just worked better with anger. But so did Tom.

"Well, whose drug problem are we talking about—mine or yours, Rosey?"

"You miserable asshole—don't you try to drag me

down into your shithole, Tom Arnold." That one thick ligament of hate that pulls the back of your brain so tight against your neck, you think it's gonna snap like a window shade, fly up, and pop you square into a place of no return gave me the shakes all over and I had to leave. I stopped making sense.

I decided, I'm gonna do something good for myself. I took a two-week vacation in Hawaii with my girlfriend. My children (whom Bill had the rights to through Christmas) had become incorrigible at this point—the victims of bad parenting and L.A. Miserable, hurt, demoralized, and in need of anything tangible that could mark some kind of progress—a tan, for God's sake—I beat it to Hawaii, trade winds, red dirt, and a big crying jag–luau for one.

I used to think Mexican music was the worst goddamned music in the world until I came to Hawaii. Even the modern folk and rock groups sound the same, like the singer is getting a tetanus shot in some ass muscle with a square needle. And the beach scene. Oh, boy. Now there's something to look forward to. It was humiliating to walk down to the beach in a swimsuit—I weighed about sixty pounds more than I do at this writing. Lying on the beach in a bathing suit with everyone knowing who you are and how fat you are is blue-chip humiliation, let me tell you. People took pictures of me while I'm lying there as if it wasn't humiliating enough just to go out of the hotel.

And then the tourists: "Hey—I know who you are."
My favorite line was from this old bastard. Guy says,
"Hey—you're not who I think I am, are ya?" I said,
"Well, I don't know. Who do you think you are?"

"That Susanna, on TV."

"Oh, yeah, you're Susanna!"

"I thought so!"

Yeah, I went to Maui, one of the most beautiful
places on earth, then holed up in my hotel room. I may
as well have been in Detroit. What I did most, besides get
high, was call Tom in the middle of the night, ostensibly
to get advice about my kids. (Incidentally, my girlfriend
told me she was instructed by Arlyne and my sisters
to make sure that I didn't call Tom. They saw their opening. With Tom banished to sleepless nights on anti-
inflammatory medication to lessen the effects of a mur-
derous withdrawal from cocaine, well, maybe he just
might be out of their hair once and for all.) My daughter
Jessica was staying at Bill's, pissed off at me and not taking my calls.

"You gotta call Jessica, she's at Bill's house and I
know he doesn't watch her. She's gonna sneak out and
I'm really, really afraid," I fretted to Tom, until someone
put an end to that, too.

"You know what?" Tom said to me through the pot,
and the time zones, and the oceanic hiss in the line.
"You can't call me anymore when you're high. I can't
handle it."

"Well, isn't that a kick in the ass."

"Look, Rosey," Tom said in a low, placid voice, "I'm gonna get sober for myself. I don't know what that means, but I'm not gonna be able to be around you at all if you keep using." Boring. After being the caretaker, the emotional janitor, for so long, here for once, the tables were turned. After a long silence: "Okay, I'll quit, too," I said.

"And, we're *gonna* get married," I decided then and there.

"We are?"

"Well, yeah. You want to, don't you?" Now I was worried, like they'd Clockwork Oranged him, or something, made him incapable of doing anything irresponsible. And marrying me was right up there, a veritable Stones tour of irresponsibility.

"Hell, yeah. Soon as I get out," Tom shouted and finally I recognized him by it—part of him was back.

But how dare I call him up in rehab, wasted on pot, making demands, when I was the one who drove him there to get help. And two things do me in: one's chocolate cake, the other's hypocrisy. So I had my little swansong binge, toked up the rest of my pot (dumping your shit down the crapper in an impulse of righteousness happens on Sunday-morning TV, but rarely in real life and certainly not in Maui), then went smokeless, got myself straight, which was no little feat. The reason, after all, that I liked to smoke pot was because it really shut down a lot of voices to the point where I'd only hear One. In the end, I had to shut her down, too.

Visiting Tom became some kind of Jungian descent/ catharsis. Each time I walked through the doors of that place I was never the same person I saw through the glass on the way out. The first time I came breech-loaded with resentment for Tom, whom I blamed for all my confusion, disenfranchisement, and pervading dread. I was alone because of him, people hated me because of him, and so on. We had a major battle right there in front of Tom's therapist. I tried to storm out, but the therapist convinced me to stay. She had a film he thought I might be interested in seeing.

"I'm not staying—I don't need to be here," I snapped, but after I made a fool of myself making that clear to everyone, I ended up staying. The film was about addiction. As I watched, I came to realize that I was using food as a substance, the way people used drugs and alcohol. I heard that drug abuse and food disorders can be traced back to sexual abuse. That was about all I could take in one sitting. I had to get out of there—I wanted to be anywhere else but there. Something inside of me started to shake me. I had no pot to quiet it; it shook louder and louder.

One of the reasons Tom figured he used drugs so much was to forget, to screen out, to hold back some of the childhood memories he's had to live with. While he detoxed, he also underwent some intense psychiatric therapy. Tom's mother (the biggest, baddest biker bitch who ever shaved her legs with a hunting knife) gave him his first beer when he was fourteen. By the time she was twenty-one, she'd been divorced four times. He lived with her for a short spell and the day he moved in she laid down the law: "Well, here's the rules: You can screw whoever you want, you can have your hair as long as you want it, and here's a beer. Relax." She and her boyfriend made Tom the drummer in their band so they could get drunk at the gigs and he could drive them all home. Tom, you see, was the Daniel Boone of alternative lifestyles.

"Something really awful happened to me when I was a boy," he told me after we hugged and ragged on each other on this visit. Tom's mother was an alcoholic. She'd abandoned the family, and he was living with his father. When he was seven, he went to visit her. She had some boyfriends at the house, all of them drunk and carousing. They locked Tom in the trunk of a car, then pissed on it. In the darkness, he could hear them laughing, he could hear the sound of their piss trickling across the trunk.

I went home that night, staggered by Tom's revelation. That was the first night that I remembered something about myself. I had my sister on one line and Tom on hold on the other. This image that I had carried with me my entire life that used to scare me in my sleep, in the dark, when I was alone—the maniac face—was always there, but I never knew why. This time, it wouldn't stop, wouldn't go away. It was blurred at first, like a bucket filled with roots and broken eggs, scrawled over in smudges of red. But it got clearer and clearer, all the parts of the picture began to behave, go to their wicked corners where they could do more harm in harmony, the hand coming down into a cheek, the lipstick crawling across a taunting mouth, then it resolved into my mother, her face matching against the maniac face, and I just lost it.

"Oh, my God! My God," I cried to my sister. "It's Mom! It's Mom, Geraldine! It's Mom!"

Geraldine tried to talk me down. "You never did it to your kids, Rose, you're a good mother. You never did it to your kids. You never did anything horrible like that." When someone's nice to you, after or when you've been abused, you tend to take the smallest kind thing that they've done for you and make the world out of it. My sister did care for me, and was comforting at the time, but she knew everything. She was at the big family confrontation in Las Vegas; she had her own secrets, her own gallery of maniacal faces.

"You can come here," Tom, waiting on the other line, invited. I got in the car and drove, the miles peeling back the lid over my memory, all these images flooding in. I remembered my mother's sadism, and how much abuse she put me through—a certain kind of abuse until I was old enough to talk, and then something ritualistic, sickening and sadistic. I came home from school one day to find her covered with catsup, lying on the floor like she was dead. I started to scream and then she got up and

sneered, "It's catsup, you idiot." Once, she pulled a
kitchen knife on me and threatened to kill me if I didn't
get to my grandma's house real quick. When I was three
or four, she liked to have me strike nude poses with her
in various sexual positions. And there was touching, but
not of the kind of healthy, loving families, no. You don't
become uncomfortable with touching unless it's the kind
that you can't understand, the kind of touching your parents wouldn't let you watch on TV or movies, but ironically was fine in our house. It was called tickling, but it
somehow always found its way south.

The mental torture was probably worse—at the
time—because that I understood. If anyone ever said
something about me, be it true or false, my mother always took their side. I'd scream "It isn't true," until my
throat was raw. "Shut up," she'd tell me and choke me
by covering my nose and mouth. There was this confus-
ing collusion between her and everyone who wanted to
hurt me. She'd make it possible for them to hurt me, then
say, "What's the matter with you? Why do you make up
these stories? Why do you lie?" Any time I'd ever tell a
school counselor (in those days, they would contact your
parents instead of the police or child protection agencies),
it would get back to my mother and it was always,
"You're crazy. Why do you make stuff up like that? It
didn't *happen*." But of course, it all *did* happen.

There was this boy who used to chase me home
from school, grab me, and lock me in his garage all the

time. His parents were German immigrants and his father had been in the S.S. I was in the second or third grade at the time and I told my mother that he had done these things, that he beat me up, bullied me, terrorized me.

"Well, we have to show him that Jews aren't bad," my mother decided, so she hired him to work in our house. She brought him to work in our *fucking house*! One of the first things he did was offer to teach me how to ride a bike, which, ignoring my apprehensions, my mother thought was a wonderful idea.

"Okay, pedal," he said, acting nice and nurturing. Then, when Mom disappeared, he'd aim the bike at a wall, without having taught me how to use the brakes. He let me hit a lot of walls before that lesson rolled around. I wouldn't really know if he was being mean to me or not because I was already trained not to see or feel or know. Mother let him work in our house until one day, when she was pulling weeds in the front yard, she saw his reflection in the door behind her—making a face as if he were about to strangle her. *Then* she fired him.

We'd go for walks or walk to the store. "That's where the rapists are." Mom would point at some shadowy spot, or between some building, or, when that didn't work, she'd point at the neighbor's apartment door. "That's where the rapist is. And he likes to hurt little girls, so you better watch out." Then she'd lock me out in the hall.

Dad? He didn't care. He'd be gone for days at a

time. We'd either find him in a pool hall, drunk, or some other place where he didn't belong, but fit in well. When he was gone, she'd sit me up on a counter. Then she'd beat me with a dish towel or her bare hand.

"Your father's a bastard, isn't he?" she'd demand.

"No . . ."

"What'd'you mean 'No'?" And she'd whack me with the towel again, until I agreed with her. "And his mother's out of her goddamned mind, right? RIGHT?" If I said yes, she'd beat me too. No logic to anything.

When I got to the detox center I found Tom and I told him what I remembered, right out there in the hall among all these detoxing fellow junkies. And they all were wonderful. They put their arms around me, held me, told me it would be all right. These strangers with problems of their own had real compassion for me. I sobbed so hard, I couldn't breathe.

Shattered and cracked. Every brain wave feels like a brain wave. Nothing comes in connected to anything else. Just loose thoughts and noises of the world. Closing my eyes I see the imprint of the corner I was staring into. "Who's there?" I think and I dart and fly all around but no one answers. Everyone is still asleep. No one knows me. I'm alone and so I realize after a while that I am a child. A child who feels no hope, no sanctity. Just hears the world's noises and far-off birds between the cars and planes. It's a big hum, but somehow the tweets are even louder. Yes, I hear the birds louder. Now shifting, I hear the cars only. Closing down parts of my brain, it senses as a gift I have learned to be given. I'm so embarrassed.

The dead will not leave me to live. They are monitoring and following me on my climb away from them. They call to me at night with their waxy, sour breath to rejoin them again for more pain to allow them access again to my blood and muscle. They call themselves my victims; I have abandoned them. I go crazy, all the way crazy at the evil they have given home to and want at times to reverently scratch out my eyes and ears to find heaven. To find quiet and peace in a place that doesn't hurt, curdle, or burn. At those times, big gaps open up and I seek a cranny for my own. In there I can hear nothing but the noises of the world. No one can call me out. I am shut up, shored, and folded—gone. Then soon after I shift. I will be able to speak again. Who will attach to my tongue?

Here is the poet. My name is Evangelina. I am so old and possessed, ensnared by despair and time lost. I stand in the rain in diaphanous fabric, my eyes hollow and full. I have no pupils because light cannot enter or escape. I am too dense inside my own matter. Was I a star who fell to the wrong earth in a puddle and became evaporating vapors that were unable to rise? My feet are webbed and under the earth. I am stationary and cannot descend. I am the dream world where all the monsters never sleep.

HONEYMOONING

IN THE

INFERNO

"You guys are different. You guys go ahead and get married," Nancy, Tom's therapist, assured us. According to popular theory, you're not supposed to have relationships for a year after you get sober, but we were "different." I'm not certain what she meant by that, but to this day I thank her for putting herself out on a limb—of a very brittle tree.

We still had the January 20 date in mind. My divorce from Bill would be final on the eighteenth—but not until some administrative constipation almost delayed the final date for another week.

"I don't care. I wanna be married on the twentieth," I told my lawyer.

"Roseanne, you'll be a bigamist then. Is that what you want?" He meant it as a rhetorical question but I sure as hell didn't take it that way.

"I'm married on that date. GET IT. I don't care what you have to do. DO IT."

Tom got out of rehab on the sixteenth and decided to get his sea legs in the sober world by planning a wedding in three days, a proposition that would land most mortals back in intensive care with morphine patches covering every inch of their bodies. Tom, who, if you described as "hyperactive," it would mean he's having a sluggish day, Tom, a sugar-rush personified, pulled the whole thing off.

And he did it without sleep. Fresh out of detox, he was clean and sober, but his metabolism was haywire. When he was using, the cocaine told him when he could sleep; now he had to tell himself, and it wasn't easy. As a result, I had the only twenty-four-hour handyman. While the rest of us slept (or tried to, depending on what power tool Tom was using), he planed doors, fixed broken appliances, replaced faucet washers. And when he ran out of things to fix, he'd do whatever he could to wake me up so he'd have someone to talk to, like he did one night before the wedding.

"Honey—are you up?" Tom was kneeling next to me, shining one of those big-ass, hungry man flashlights in my face.

"What?" I moaned.

"I hear something in the walls, honey."

"Goddamn it, Tom, you're hallucinating. Now either come to bed or go fix something," I told him. For the next three nights he came in, insisting he'd heard something, and I figured he was just overwhelmed by all the changes he was going through—marriage, sobriety, fatherhood, and of course all those six-foot-tall termites gnawing on his ass every day in the writers room.

Our little informal wedding at the Benedict Canyon house ended up with thirty guests and fifty bodyguards. People were hanging in the trees, on our roof, while the number of helicopters hovering and swooping in for pictures equaled the number used in *Platoon*.

Like a pigeon that pecks at a colored dot a thousand times without giving up, I was still trying to get close to my family. We invited both families, Tom's and my own, out to our wedding in Los Angeles. Nobody gave us any wedding presents, the rationale being that their sheer presence was a gift, which I gotta say is a real stretch, in light of the fact that less than a month before I had had that electrical storm of memories about my mom.

The wedding went well, considering the company. Tom had a beard now, which he grew during rehab and which made him look like a World Federation wrestler in a suit. The idiots who sold me my wedding dress forgot to remove that chunk of antitheft plastic and even Jenny, with all of her lock-picking expertise, couldn't remove it. We had to cut the lace around it. The dress looked as if a dog had taken a bite out of it. And if you're into symbolism, we found a rat floating in the swimming pool. My son Jake, Tom's father, and Tom's AA sponsor were best men. My sisters were matrons of honor, but refused to stand next to Tom and me until I hollered at them to get their frilly asses up there.

I wrestled briefly with the idea of confronting my mother about my memories of abuse. The thing is, when you first get your memories, you spend a good deal of time doubting them, challenging yourself, i.e., was it really real? You know they are, but you're dying to give the womb you crawled out of the benefit of the doubt. Also, I was in prime time denial—oh, whatever my mother did, it was a long time ago and she was messed up, she's been to therapy, I can just put it behind me now, so she can't be like that anymore. So I kept quiet while my parents rode around in limousines.

The honeymoon had its moments. We spent our wedding night at the Beverly Hills Hotel, then had our limo driver take us to Duke's up on Sunset Boulevard for breakfast. When we came out, the limo was gone for some reason, so we hitchhiked back to the hotel. The tabloids missed out on a great picture there! Geraldine agreed to watch the kids, which meant they were able to sneak out and go to watch *The Rocky Horror Picture Show*. The tabloids did, however, follow us down to Mexico, where we were ambushed by photographers at the airport, while a big fat sheriff stood by and let these shutterbugs (vermin, to be exact) blind us with their flashes.

Still, for the most part, the trip was an absolute gas mainly because we scrapped the original plan to stay in Acapulco for two weeks because of paparazzi, for an all-out nostalgia Baedeker. Taking advantage of the rented jet we had at our disposal, we flew to see Tom's grandparents, then to see Brandi in Austin. We joined the Mile High Club. After that, we swung up to Minneapolis to hang out with friends and finally wound up sleeping in Tom's childhood bed at his parents' house in Iowa. It was all really even better than what we had planned.

What kind of became a real memory spoiler was that while Tom and I fed each other wedding cake on our wedding night at the Beverly Hills Hotel, my father was molesting my daughter Jess.

Tom's first day out of rehab, just days before the wedding, was a busy one. That was it for a lot of assholes; he cleaned house. Jeff Harris went first. We brought in Jay Daniel and allowed Jeff to sit out the remainder of his year in office—it's called "saving face," which, when translated, means he got paid for the rest of the season and didn't have to do a thing. I wouldn't let him be in the cast picture; he had to have his picture taken by himself, which was kind of sad, but so was Leona Helmsley's first night in jail and we all got over that.

Next to go was Barry Hirsch, my big-time Hollywood lawyer. I had talked to him about my problems on the show, called him one night, while Tom listened in on the other line.

"Just let me know because I'll file bankruptcy for you," Barry said. Barry was obviously trying to scare me, so I wouldn't bother him on vacation again, a tactic that didn't sit too well with Tom, who went ballistic.

"Why you motherfucker—you don't ever talk to a woman who's already *been* bankrupt and has three kids about filing bankruptcy. Don't you know anything more than this about helping her? You better get your worthless ass in gear. What kind of bullshit is this? She's gotta file bankruptcy now? Are you fucking out of your mind?" There was a long silence until Barry cleared his throat, then replied:

"Well, I didn't mean that exactly . . . uh, that she'd have to, you know . . ." Tom slammed down the phone.

Tom called Arlyne next from Mexico while we were on our honeymoon. "Arlyne," he said, "clean out your locker." Then he sent her an official fax saying she was no longer my manager. My new manager was Tom.

The first thing that came out of anyone's mouth was

"Everything was all right until Mister Tom Arnold came along." Tom was the one who finally said enough's enough.

I was mad at first. The night we flew back from Mexico to Texas on our honeymoon, we had a huge fight on the airplane. "That's my goddamn family—you can't do that to my family." He said, "What have they done for you? They treat you like shit and you just keep excusing them for it." You mean I had a choice?

On our honeymoon, we did a lot of talking about our futures, the kids, the show, everything, since neither of us had used for a couple of months so we actually had clear heads.

"You know, everything your sisters do, they do out of resentment," Tom said at one point.

He reached this conclusion after my sister, Geraldine, decided to quit working for the "Roseanne" show, maintaining that she "needed her freedom." She hired an old friend to take her place at a fraction of her salary, the balance of which she kept.

Tom and I had been developing this cartoon, "Little Rosey," based on my life and including members of my family. I'd been talking about it for quite a while and finally got to a point where the whole thing was coming together. Geraldine announced that she would write, direct, and produce the cartoon, which was a nice thought since we were busy with the show, but Geraldine wasn't

Walt Disney. At the end of the time limit we gave her, she had no script, no outline, no nothing, as usual. When the deadline came and the producers came down from Canada, she had a total of eight words on paper: "This is the story about a little girl," or something like that, if it was even that descriptive, but that was Geraldine.

Tom's problem with Geraldine came mainly from her use of the word "monies." She'd say, "Certain monies are to be paid . . ." and Tom would load an imaginary gun and point it at his own temple, then pull the trigger. When she droned on and on about "interfacing with people," he was tempted to find a real one. Geraldine and I first interfaced when she was just a newborn and I was four.

"You have a sister," they told me and I'm, like, what? Because they never told me they were having a baby. I just thought this was so cool and I had to see her. I went into Geraldine's room. I was tickling her feet, when the second-hand bassinet somehow collapsed. My mother rushed into the room, shrieking like she had just downed a glass of napalm: "My God, My God! SHE'S TRYING TO KILL MY BABY! SHE'S TRYING TO KILL MY BABY!" She grabbed me by the arm, swung me around, and flung me into a wall.

The November before my wedding, my sister Stephanie was going into one of her depressions. I wanted to do something to lift her spirits, to show her that I loved and supported her. Maybe if she came to stay with me for a while and got out of her present surroundings, it might speed her emotional recovery, so I called her.

"You know, I want you to come and spend some time up in Benedict Canyon. You've never been up here. Why don't you come up for the weekend?"

"Well, I have to tell you something," she shot back. "I cannot ever come to see your house. Because it really makes me mad that you have a nice house. I can't help it, that's the way I feel, and I'm never gonna come and see your house."

To understand how my sister could make a comment like that it's important to remember that we were basically a dysfunctional family, picture-perfect in every possible scenario of S and M, having a love/hate relationship with everyone and everything.

A lot of Stephanie's percolating hate for me was really for Mom and Dad, classic aggression-transfer. I was like her parent. She was eleven years younger than me. My mom literally gave her over to me to raise, and I did. I brought her to Denver, supported her for years, dragged her out of a bad relationship, then brought her again to live with me in Los Angeles. I usually let Stephanie's bitter little comments like that go (up until recently, I just felt sorry for everyone but me), but this one hurt, this one cut deep, for obvious reasons. The mothers-torn-from-their-babies theme was a popular one in our family; it worked on me like a charm. After all, I was used to being the family scapegoat.

This is what happens to survivors like me. The whole sick family always expects you to be the emotional handyman, the Mrs. Fix-it, the person who can hold the whole rickety, corroded mess together. When I went into show business and actually began to make money, it was assumed that I would take care of my family forever. When I was living in Encino and making some decent money, my father wanted me to buy a duplex so that he and my mother could live on one side and my family could live on the other. So he wouldn't have to work. And I was gonna do it! I always had a guest house for my sisters, so they wouldn't have to worry about rent.

Yeah, my sisters really were supportive of me and my children in the beginning, even though they occasionally hit them and berated them while I was at work, or decided to move out just when my work started to accelerate because they had their own needs, too, and couldn't be expected to baby-sit all the time. Even though I put up my house to finance my sisters' education. But neither of them wanted to work, really.

When I began to deal with my own incest issues, I had to cut my parents and sisters off. That was the best thing I ever did. Because it wasn't going to be my fault anymore; it would be their own. They got so angry they engaged a lawyer who threatened to sue me. And that's all part of it—they were so angry about the money.

But I'll tell you what. Karma is money, money is shit, and the three all go together. I have had no contact with my family for almost four years now, and these four years have been the most productive, healing, and happy years of my life.

After the wedding, we had some time to spend on two projects, one major, the other minor—that is, if you're not afraid of rats. Tom kept hearing noises in the middle of the night, and it turned out to be a huge colony of rodents living between the walls and in the attic. We discovered them after everyone in the house blamed each other for smelling bad. Tom eventually traced the odor to the attic, where he discovered hundreds of rotting rat carcasses. At least they don't eat their own, which is more than you can say about network executives.

Our larger idea (though equal in the odor department) was salvaging the whole cartoon project. The thought from the start was to keep it in the family monies-wise, as Geraldine would say, as a sort of nice little cash cow for everyone. The deal was that each member of the family would be paid one dollar for his or her story—a formality so that my brothers and sisters could benefit from licensing fees, all the merchandising, i.e., dolls, T-shirts, toys, lunch boxes, and whatever else.

Geraldine would own 100 percent of her character.

Everyone stood to make some guaranteed money, and there were other deals as well. A deal with Burger King for a million dollars was in the offing; Geraldine's share of that deal alone was $100,000. It meant that all of our likenesses would appear on Burger King cups and posters.

The big stickler was that no one trusted Tom and they all wanted money up front before they'd sign the deal. This was when we were all getting along. No one would sign releases for the series, or at least no one would tell the truth about signing them. My mother, that kidder, that ham, that life of the party, whoopie-cushion, hand-buzzer practical joker, told me that her signed release was in the mail which she had said ten thousand times before, and I fell for it then, too.

When it never arrived, I called her. "To be honest, with you, Roseanne, we don't trust you and Tom with our characters and what you're gonna do with them," my mom told me. Assuming the worst, that I planned on making them the king and queen of the sadomasochistic realm of the snake people who ate human flesh and had sex with mountain goats, the fact that this was a Saturday morning cartoon for children had completely whizzed over her head.

"Look," Tom tried to reason with her, "you probably *all* think you're going to become big cartoon stars from this but let's face it—people will be watching because 'Little Rosey' will be on the show, not because 'Little Stephanie,' or 'Little Geraldine,' are on, know what I mean?" When we called her about the cartoon, Little Stephanie had her own idea altogether.

"I don't want any percentage of your show. If you and Tom really want to help me, you'll give me thirty-five thousand dollars cash right now, so I can finish school." Everyone who's famous has relatives who ask them for money. I have done a lot of research, and for some reason, it's almost always the sum of $35,000, *no shit*!

Tom was sitting right there; we were listening on speakerphone.

"You're not gonna get any money," Tom spoke up, shaking his head. Steph, the Sugar Ray Leonard of story-changing, commenced with the fancy footwork.

At one time or another, I've heard from every single member of my family—some were repeat offenders—that they were suffering from some life-threatening illness. They never really do have it, though, and they're all gonna outlive me. *I'm* the one who's probably got cancer. A whole damn victory garden of it growing in me if all that stuff about stress is even half true.

"Are you gonna at least come and visit me in the hospital, Rose?" Steph cried at what sounded like a rate of $10,000 a tear.

"No, uh, I won't be visiting you in the hospital. You've really fucked me over. For the last time." One of the first times was when she and her husband moved out to L.A. Ira, her husband, was a carpenter and the plan was for him to come to work on the "Roseanne" show, building sets. I had four months left on my lease—I was about to move to Encino, our first home in California— and I offered Steph and Ira the place. In a matter of three months, they casually demolished it, costing me thousands of dollars' worth of repairs, but as always, they figured I'd take care of it. I always did before. I was rich, right?

"So are you saying that you're never gonna talk to me again?" Steph sniffed.

"If she doesn't say it, I'll say it for her," Tom chimed in. "You treat Rosey like shit and I'm not gonna let you talk to her anymore. Them days are over." Everything was fine until Mr. Tom Arnold . . .

After all the haggling, we missed another deadline and it hurt us with the network. We had to change every character at the last minute, using my own kids as prototypes and Tom and I as the prototypical parents. All this chaos ultimately cost us the show. It was one of my quieter failures.

OH, SAY, CAN YOU SING?

om Werner bought the Padres from Ray Kroc, the
evil genius who harnessed the working potential of
the third world ("Welco' to Madonna, can I ta'
your odor?") and drove modern man to his knees with
the aroma of vat grease. Tom, my husband, was in a
meeting with Tom Werner, the two of them shooting the
breeze, when Tom Werner mentioned one of the Padres'
promotional nights. They were honoring women who
had to work for a living called "Working Women Night."

"Why don't you have Roseanne sing the National

Anthem?" Tom suggested. "She's America's most famous working woman, right?" Fabulous idea, Tom Werner agreed. Fabulous.

The Padres sent their private plane for us—me, Tom, my son, Jake, and my daughter, Jessica. On the way down, I dutifully ran through the anthem a few times, remembering what Michael Bolton said about the vocal chords being nothing more than a muscle and if you don't exercise them, they'll get flabby or something. I sang it straight, reverently, the way it was meant to be sung, but Jake had second thoughts.

"I don't know, Mom . . . I'm kinda worried about all those people who might think you're making fun of the country."

"Nonsense. They aren't gonna think that. Why would they think that?"

"Well, you're not really a singer and I'm afraid for you." I was touched by his concern, but Jake needed some education here.

"People know I'm not a singer, but I have a decent voice, I can carry a tune and that's okay. I'm an American, I'm a patriot. Hey, if Whitney Houston can hit a clinker now and then, so can I, right? Besides, those are my people down there, Jake."

"Good speech, Rosey." Tom clapped.

The thing about Jack Murphy Stadium is it lacks paint. You go to Dodger Stadium and it's like Cirque du Soleil, the seats all orange and yellow and blue against

the red infield clay and the lush green grass. You just
don't get that feeling of mortal combat or going into second with your spikes up. Jack Murphy Stadium is different. With all its concrete and imposing overhangs and
cantilevers, it looks like the coliseums in those Kirk
Douglas movies where they crucify people upside-down
or throw them to the lions. It's a big, in-your-face place
and walking onto the field to meet the players, I could
feel my vocal chords knotting up into a fist. The players
made me feel at home. They thought it was really great
that I was gonna sing—*everyone* thought it was great
that I was gonna sing. Humorous. They all thought it
was humorous. They'd heard me do my Vegas act and
were surprised at the quality of my voice, how good it
was, and blah, blah, blah. It was supposed to be this cute,
kitschy thing and in that spirit, a bunch of the ballplayers
said, "Hey, when you're done singing, you oughta grab
your crotch and spit."

"Oh, yeah, honey—that would be great! You gotta
do it." Tom was right in there with 'em. Tom, who ate
live goldfish and never met a joke too tasteless to tell or
a gag too risky to perform.

"Oh, that's so funny," another ballplayer (no longer
with the club, I might add) agreed. "People will love that
if you do that." And right there I should've known better.
Anyone who looks like he's got a spare baseball stored in
his cheek and whose teeth are blacked out by chewing to-
bacco doesn't know what's funny and certainly doesn't

know what looks stupid. But what do I know? And besides, it was like this big classroom dare and I ain't so shy when it comes to that dare stuff. The classroom just turned out to be the whole United States this time.

By now you may have guessed that there were a number of things I hadn't accounted for. First of all, I found out I'd be singing *between* games, meaning the whole stadium (which was a sellout at 64,000) was already working on four hundred tons of beer. And San Diego, which is sometimes called the "Cradle of California Civilization," is a rather conservative place, with all its military bases and Mister Pete Wilson once running the show. Most of the blacks in the city are on the baseball team.

As I walked toward the field to sing, the 64,000 fans went absolutely wild, screaming and cheering. I could see the ones near the railings and let me tell you, alcohol poisoning was a definite maybe. A lot of angry, peptic smiles, the kind you see at awards shows on the faces of the losers. I passed one section that was completely shielded from the sun and still most of them were squinting, a few literally cross-eyed. The half-drunk ones looked the most dangerous. These were the ones who in reality wanted to make sausage out of my ass and fry it up at the next tailgate party but sort of just went along with the cheering since they were outnumbered. For the time being, anyway.

So I get led to my spot and the usher hands me the mike and motions for me to start singing.

"Whenever you're ready, Mrs. Arnold."

"Wait a minute. Isn't there gonna be any organ music accompanying me?" He just shrugged and walked backwards really fast. But there was no music, no accompaniment, and worst of all, no note to even start me out on. Just 64,000 people waiting for the anthem to be sung, goddamnit, so they can sit down again, many of them already beginning to do so. I never thought about asking for music—I'm not a professional singer, I didn't know. And I didn't know you had to start out in a really low key if you had any hope of making it through the song. And I still didn't know until I sang the first five words and when I hit that note on "see," my voice cracked and wavered like a yodeler singing through a tubal ligation. The more I tried to steady the note, the more the bottom dropped out of it—you talk about your candle in the wind, boy, I chased that note all over the scale and back and still never caught up with it. And then I couldn't even hear myself because one of those military bases picked that time to scramble their bombers and all I could think was oh, my God, I started too high, I started too high.

Then I realized it wasn't bombers flying overhead, it was booing. They were booing me! First the half-drunk, then the drunk, a rumble of boos spreading like they were doing the wave with booing. I kept singing and the notes kept getting higher and higher to the point where I could see them in my mind, two floors above me but where there were supposed to be stairs there was only a piece of rope with a note on it that said, "What the hell have you done?" Now all I wanted to do was run and hide, run to the infield, dig a hole, and bury myself in it (there were others who would've gladly obliged), just quit and say I'm sorry that I ever thought I could sing this bloody song and leave. But I knew I couldn't (show business is masochism and penance, among other things).

I looked over at Tom and even he had this awful look of doom rimmed in his eyes, like this is the captain speaking and we're out of fuel. By the time I reached the "land of the free" line, I was no longer singing; instead, I was screaming at the level of the Khrushchev "We will bury you" speech and I had no idea what I sounded like because the booing was loud enough to drown me out. By the end of the song I looked up and all I saw were 64,000 Edvard Munch faces, all adenoids and Adam's apples. The whole place was booing me, even the orphaned kids there on a field day, even the nuns. That was the last straw. Fuck 'em all.

On the last note, I decided to punish them with my voice and made the loudest noise I've ever made in my life, a holler so loud that the whole section of navy personnel flinched, so loud that when I saw it on videotape later, the camera shook, so loud that I stretched a muscle in my neck.

I saw Tom, shaking his head, like for God's sake,

don't go through with it but I did, I had to. I grabbed my crotch and spit, trying to make it at *least* funny at the end, but they weren't buying that. Now it looked as though some folks had actually turned purple jeering me and others had that little forward lean in their posture betraying a willingness to charge the field at the sight of the first one crazy enough to do so. And we couldn't leave just yet because Tom was supposed to throw out the first ball. He gamely took the mound, waving and smiling at the fans, who yelled things at him that you only hear in jail, while my kids looked at me with a mixture of pity and resignation, since they'd seen it all before—but never this loud. While poor Tom threw a perfect strike, the crowd was throwing everything they could find down on the field—hot dog wrappers, programs, paper cups, seat cushions, scorecards, popcorn boxes—everything. I was clinging to Tom when one of the Padre officials jogged toward us, dodging the hailstorm of debris.

"Would you like us to escort you back to your seats?" he said with some trepidation.

"What are you talking about?" Tom was incredulous.

"You don't . . . want to stay for the game, then—"

"Fuck, no! Get us *out of here*!"

We had to go under the building, back to the car, jump in, with everyone still screaming and going nuts. I have to say that when I was brave enough to look up, there were a lot of people going "Yay!" and laughing their asses off, probably the ones who were just completely pickled or who had any sense of humor, 'cause it's really the funniest fucking thing I ever did. After it was all over, they were laughing over there in France and in Canada. And at De Paul University, they invited me to come and sing again. I, for one, think they're the coolest college in the world.

Back on the private plane, my children were just sitting there, watching me like I had asked to have myself strapped to the front of the space shuttle in a thong, just watching me and waiting.

"Well, I'm glad that's all behind us," I said cheerfully.

As we were going to bed that night, Tom and I snuggled up to each other and turned on the news.

"Tonight . . . DISGRACE," this bitch-newscaster starts out, like the president's been caught slipping the salami to a mountain goat in the bushes on the south lawn. She reports the whole incident, with dramatic footage, and then closes with this baleful summation: "She is lucky she got off that field with her *life*." I am staggered and I shake Tom's arm:

"What are they saying? Oh, my God, listen to what they're saying? And why is it on the national news?"

"Oh, come on, come on, it'll be okay. Whole thing's gonna just roll over and die," Tom tried to assure me and switched off the light. "You'll see."

At six in the morning, the phones started ringing. By the end of the day, we got nearly two thousand calls from the press. Two thousand motherfuckers calling up. "Why'd she spit on our flag?" was the inquiry ad nauseum, thinking that I had scratched my crotch and spit on the ground because I hate this country. I mean, the worst things they can come up with for me, they always do, but that was digging at its lowest. Call after call, until I went into shock. All I did was sit up in my room and go, "Oh, my God!" and cry. The real killer was when Bob Iger called and wanted to know why I went and pulled a stunt like this now, just when everything was going so well. They were all doing my eulogy over there. And then a day after I sang, Hussein invaded Kuwait. If they wouldn't have had me all over the news, if they would've paid attention to something decent, they probably could've prevented the war.

We were living down at the beach at the time, and I was crushed. All that I had worked for looked suspect, all the gold was turning to lead, all because I had a tin ear. Jake was really sweet and tried to cheer me up with a walk on the beach.

"Mom," he says, "I have to tell you something. You think you got it bad, right? Well, just think about what they say about Richard Gere."

"You know, Jake, you're right. It's not as bad as what they say about Richard Gere." The fact of the matter, though, was that in Richard Gere's case it probably wasn't true. In mine, I *was* taking it up the ass from a bunch of weasels.

The whole thing threw me so off balance, I'd go from being really depressed to really giddy and back. I was really terrified because there was talk about sponsors pulling out of the show. The network, always there to give a few words of encouragement, took the position that, hey, whatever your rating is, well—we'll see. So there was no backup, no support, no one, and I was scared shitless for something that was just supposed to be cute.

The guy I should've listened a little harder to was Johnny Carson. Tom and I made an appearance on his show the night before we went to San Diego. I told Carson about getting to sing the anthem and he warned, "Well, you know, that's a very hard song to sing. Even opera singers have trouble with it. Whatever you do, you gotta pitch yourself low on that sucker." No kidding.

"You stay upstairs in bed," Tom instructed me. "I'll take care of everything. I'll do the talking." Everyone in the world came up to our house, every news organization, every eyewitness-news, entertainment-right-now, hard-copy, soft-core bullshit outfit you could think of came up there looking for—no, *expecting*—an answer. Tom told them all the same thing—"That's how she sings. She didn't mean any disrespect. That is how she sings"—and they just couldn't get it. We watched Jane Pauley do her show, opening with a picture of me.

"Alone and disgraced," Pauley chagrined, "she finds herself not unlike Elvis did in his final days, isolated from her people," like that, on and on until Tom finally decided to hold a press conference, with the idea that I would meet them all face to face. I wasn't about to talk to any of them, so he was left fielding the first barrage. But then it was my turn.

This is why I love Jerry Dumphy and I always invite him to all my parties. In a complete state of desperation, I turned on his newscast. Jerry went to live-remote, at Dodger Stadium, where another reporter was covering the game. They were just wrapping up the National Anthem, and this reporter turns to the camera and says, "And that, Ms. Barr, is the way the National Anthem should sound." Jerry gets that quizzical look of humility on his face and says, "Hey—has anyone there in that whole stadium there mentioned anything about freedom of speech or why, if you can burn the flag, you can't spoof the National Anthem? Has anyone talked about that?" Right on.

By then I was so spitting mad that I called the station and they put me on the air live. "I'll sing that damned song any damned time I wanna sing that song," I said over the air. At that moment it had turned in my mind into some great big mission. Hey—I don't have any bosses. I don't have any superiors. This isn't goddamn China. I'm not Anne Frank, gotta hide out because the PC police are gonna find me and kill me. I'm an

American and that is my song, too. What, only the best voices can sing that song? You gotta be Pavarotti (who sometimes lip-syncs, by the way), or Liza, or Barbra to sing the National Anthem? It's gotta be elitism if you have to have perfect pitch and be an opera singer to sing the National Anthem. And tell Bush I'd like to see his ass sing it better than I did. He's got his nerve climbing up my tailpipe right after his son leads the way in the S & L scam. You know what else? We got the only anthem that's about war and killing people. Now where's that at? Huh?

Even after my statement on Jerry Dumphy's show, it still wasn't dying down. Now it had gotten to the point where I was caught in the bushes with a Clydesdale. We decided to do a live press conference with CNN. When the *National Enquirer*'s person showed up, Tom blew his stack.

"We're not starting this press conference until that guy is out of the room. Now get out of here, you son of a bitch! I repeat, we're not starting until that asshole is out of the room!" What Tom didn't realize was that the press conference had already started, since it was a live feed—seventeen minutes of live coverage of Tom, shouting, "Get the fuck out of here! GET OUT OF HERE, YOU SHIT! I'LL THROW YOU OUT ON YOUR ASS MYSELF!" Really good PR.

Pretty soon it got so bad that people working for the "Roseanne" show—costume and set designers, makeup and wardrobe people—were being set upon by old ladies wherever they went. "You tell Roseanne she's a disgrace." "You tell Roseanne I wouldn't watch her show if it was the only program on television." Anyone who knew me, anywhere I went, sitting in a deli, whatever, I got bitched out. The Veterans of Foreign Wars started this "Boycott Roseanne" movement. Them, I can understand. They needed something to do other than ride those miniature motorcycles in Memorial Day parades and wait to get the big draft notice from the Big General in the sky. But there was an ad in *Rolling Stone* called BAN BARR FROM THE AIRWAVES and they reportedly signed up six hundred members in one day. Another guy was inventing a Roseanne doll that you could throw pins at. At the last minute he changed it to a Saddam Hussein doll. But it was meant to be me, so I was lucky that war started.

Well, I might not be the most sane person the Padres ever encountered, but I'm sure as hell not the craziest, either. Some time after my anthem-battering episode, they forwarded a letter to me from a woman who wrote, "Dear Padre management—I know that Roseanne did not mean any ill by this. I believe it was the spirit of Ray Kroc that entered her body without permission. He's been known to do these kinds of things, so please, be open-minded with Roseanne."

She signed her name, with her address and phone number, and I thought it was such a great letter, I had Tom call her up.

"Hi—this is Ray Kroc," Tom said, when he finally reached her. She started laughing right off.

"Oh, it's not you. This must be Ray Kroc, Junior."

"Yes, it is," Tom confessed. "It is Ray Kroc, Junior. And I just wanted to tell you that we read your letter and we appreciate you supporting Roseanne."

"Well, I'll tell ya what," she says. "I knew when I saw it that it was the spirit of Ray Kroc entering Roseanne, making her grab her crotch because he's been doing that to me allllllll day."

We had to wait all summer before we would know the fate of the show and naturally, I obsessed on it every day. For a while there, I actually did think it was all over for me. I was in this breath-stealing nosedive yelling, "Pull up! pull up!" in my sleep. I was worried about the ratings, how everything was gonna affect the ratings, and we still had a month to go.

"Let's just do the work. Just turn it over to God and we'll do the work," Tom said. And that's what we did. Then we went fishing the week that the show premiered for that season. When we called in for the ratings, they were the very same ratings that they always were. And it was like, thank you, God, thank you, God, thank you, God, thank you, America!

First on the hit parade was "Good Morning America," who said they were coming to where we were fishing in Iowa to "cover the huge triumph." Everyone was claiming victory, some entitled, some not. The network, for example, was now totally on my side—which is why they can all just take a fucking flying leap toward kissing my ass. Because I remember how they weren't there for me, how they treated me like a piece of shit they could toss out if they needed to.

So "Good Morning America" came out with their mobile feed to Iowa supposedly to talk about the good ratings and the success of the show.

"You make sure they ask me nothin' about the National Anthem or I'm not goin' on," I warned the producers. That fiasco was two months behind me now and the last thing Tom or I wanted was to visit that territory again. To celebrate, we went downtown and bought twin outfits for the show. We both had on red plaid shirts, overalls, big straw hats, and we carried fishing poles. "Hee Haw" time. "No, we promise—no anthem questions," the producers swore up and down and I hadn't yet had every ounce of faith in my fellow man drained from me yet, so like a dumb hick, I believed them. The host, Joan Lunden, starts in innocent enough, made some nice comments about the show, then made nice about our clothes.

"I see you're dressed like twins. So, you two catch any fish yet?" And we're all yucking up a little lake squall when Lady Nevershit yanks up the chainsaw. "You know, I just wouldn't be doing my job if I didn't mention the National Anthem," she whines, like instead of admitting that her *job* is to dive for loose change in untreated sewage, now I'm supposed to feel sorry for her because those mean old executives made her ask naughty questions. Rather than dignifying her with an answer, I clammed up and just glared into the monitor with murder in my heart, a tactic that probably would've been more effective without the Tom Sawyer outfit, but I think the guys in the remote truck got the point. Miss Broadcast News sure as hell did.

"Oh, my God, she's not going to answer!" Lunden screamed out. I just kept staring into the camera. Tom followed Lunden's lead and sat there, looking at me, with a pleasant smile on his face.

"Well," he observes, as if reading my features for the answer, "she's, uh, very grateful to her fans," then he ducked a little to get a closer look at my eyes, "and she's happy that the ratings are up, and she thanks all of you."

As soon as we went off the live feed, I got on the phone and called ABC in New York.

"I want Joan Lunden fired! I want that bitch fired!" I kinda lost it there for a while.

"Well, you don't really have any domain over the news," they tried to reason with me.

"Yeah? I'm the number one fucking thing on this network and it'd be number three if it wasn't for me. You'd think they can have some respect for me. Now I want that old hag Joan Lunden fired!" I was summarily dismissed. WELL. The nerve.

Then I got a taste of my own medicine, aka

"Howdy, pard." Everywhere we went people were singing the anthem off-key. We went to the Rose Bowl. I knew what I was in store for—are you kidding? Beer, college kids, and yahoos meant we'd be serenaded in song, lyrics courtesy of Francis Scott Key, and I didn't want to go, but Iowa was playing and Tom's a Hawkeye through and through.

"OHHHH, SAY, CAN YOU SEE?" as we walked through the aisles. Tom got in this guy's personal space and threatened to throw him into a nearby pond after threatening to kill him first.

"Oh, yeah?" the guy growled. "Is your wife gonna be singing the National Anthem? 'Cause if she is, I'm gonna kill *you*." A bunch of folks had to separate them, then we had to watch that stupid football game, which Iowa went and lost anyway.

It was relentless. At a restaurant in L.A., this Drunker-Than-Shit, sitting behind our table, singing "Neau say cnnn nueu three?" shrieking like a cat in heat, trying to be funny for his wife and another couple. Tom gets up, whirls around to their table, grabs the guy by the collar, and lifts him out of his shoes. "Do you want me to take you outside and end your life?" Tom's shaking the guy like a mop head. "Stop singing that. I'm here with my family and we do not wish to be disturbed." The guy makes this delirious drunk laugh and starts singing it again. This time Tom leans down and grabs the guy's wife.

"Do you want me to break your husband's neck right here, or will you shut him up? Because I will. I'll kick his ass in through his head."

"Honey, shut up. SHUT UP," the wife commands. "JUST SHUT UP."

The anthem thing still stayed with me, like lingering flu, but after six months of being linked to that damned song as if it was a part of me, like Judy Garland and "Somewhere Over the Goddamn Rainbow," I was beginning to at least face it.

During the Iraqi War, Tom and I did our bit, entertaining the wives of the troops of Desert Storm. The wives wanted to see me, anthem be damned, which was really cool. We went to bases all over California and did stand-up, with an assist, if you could call it that, from Delta Burke's husband. He calls me up, all blustery with military jargon and shit, and says, "Roseanne, I thought you should know. I've spoken to the generals and the people at these bases, and I've let them know that it was just a joke that went bad." Uh-huh. Like, what else could it be? Just some big Communist Bitch that stormed onto the field and grabbed the mike, I'll show you, you fucking Christian heathens! "I've made it clear to them all," Major Dad continues, like he's my commanding officer or something, "that you will behave in accordance with the traditions of honor to our flag and National Anthem." Then we went to these places to entertain the wives and they weren't upset about the anthem. They were just upset. I saw this black woman in the front row who wouldn't stop bitching about the war.

"You wanna come up here and bitch into the microphone?" I asked her.

"I sure do." It was really hard to understand her because she was Deep Southern but we all got the message. "They say we're goin' back there. Well, mah mayin ain't goin' back there. If he bring his ass home in one piece, he *stayin'*, he ain't goin' back there. Not mah mayin." All the women were so cool. And the generals liked us so much because we did all these things for free that they asked us to be in the Desert Storm parade.

So Tom and I were in the parade, in some kind of simple twist of fate, but we may as well have been Aziz and his wife. There were close to two million people at the parade, and everywhere I looked guys were giving us the finger or making monkey faces at us. There were old guys in uniform who saw us coming and would literally turn their backs on us—just turn the other way. So I just kept looking at the kids in the front row, who kept cheering, "Roseanne! Roseanne!" Others would razz us with those deep, terrible, guttural booing sounds that came out, "BBBBEEEAAUUUUW!" nearing beer-belch sound barrier. And then there was the religious left (à la Fran Leibowitz) shouting, "Roseanne, you traitor! Why're you in that parade, you traitor!"

"Hey, buddy, have a nice day." Tom waved, like a baseball star. Baseball star and prom queen, yeah, that was us.

So I tried to face it all, with millions of people watching me sweat, watching me squirm like a caterpillar put on its back by some kid with a stick. Most of them weren't mad or mean, but the ones who were took up the slack nicely.

"You know, a lot of people don't come back from stuff like that," many people have remarked, trying to be Mister/Ms. Perspective. *No shit, they don't come back* and I see why! They don't *want* to. After the parade and, finally, after six long months, the big black anthem fog dissipated. To this day, though, people still sing that godawful song to me—in jest, but all the same . . . "Howdy, pard."

CHAPTER 18

THE CRITICS

What Am I Anyway, a Zoo?
By Roseanne Arnold
The New York Times, *September 30, 1990 Op-Ed*

Perusin' the news, as I have been for a while, I was surprised to find myself dissected, directed, and interjected. Feeling piqued and overly critiqued by the local/national audio-visual scriveners rushing here, arriving there, in their snoop-and-scoop mobiles, on the tracks of "The Next Big Thing and What It Means," in order to

217

*satisfy the public's itchin' for constant news gratification,
I ask: Mr. McLuhan, does mass media equal mass unconscious, or does mass unconscious beget mass media, or
does mass media belong only to those quasi-elitist folk
who feel compelled to be apologists for and/or defend
some status quo and/or personal agenda? And what
about this madonna/whore thing? Hmmm? . . . Geez, all
these critics can make a gal so nervous!*

*Newswise, I started off as a regular housewife and
before I knew it, I supposedly stood for something. At
first, I think I stood for all the latent energy and talent
that resides in ordinary folks living ordinary lives of quiet
desperation in better trailer parks everywhere.*

*Shortly thereafter, I was standing for mother, giving
a sort of postfeminist mud pie in the eye to the Super
Mom Syndrome.*

*Right after that I was standing for the Little Guy
[sic]—God bless him [sic]—who stood up against the corporate greed ogres and wrestled back some fair share,
chunk/piece of apple pie from the American collective
media unconscious and liberated it from the dessert-
hungry, unwashed masses, making TV a safer place—by
gum!—for working Americans.*

*I was also standing for fat people, the forgotten mi-
nority. And didn't we have the right to live in denial, like
everyone else? So there.*

*I read along the way that I was also standing for so-
cial folk remedies, anti-intellectualism, anti-feminism, ex-*

*mental hospital inmates, people who've cried on Barbara
Walters, women's taking over prime time in front of and
behind the camera, right-to-lifers and pro-choicers, and
let's not forget anti-manners.*

*Right after that—or was it at the same time?—I was
standing for the saying "Absolute power corrupts absolutely," representing the many women who have become
megalomaniacal dictators.*

*Around the fall, I stood for Queen of Tabloid Amer-
ica, which no one reads. I believe that no one does, too.
Really. I think it's just like the 100th monkey syndrome—
more glorious proof of our human evolution. Like when
that one monkey started washing his food, and all over
the world, within days, thousands more monkeys started
to make likewise. That's how it goes: one person believes
that I'm the ceremonial gypsy goddess human sacrifice of
a Mexican death cult and soon everyone else just knows
it, too—even though they don't even go to the supermar-
ket.*

*Somewhere I stood for all the anger at Mother ev-
erywhere, too, and the separation anxiety from being
kicked out of the womb, and how dare I have one, or use
anything attached to it? Good mothers just say no! I
stood for the traditional American family and later, its
demise.*

*I stood for sex, too: fat, sweatin', darkly Oedipal,
ground-grabbin' sex like the boys like it around the Mid-
west, below the corn belt, sex that is all subtext.*

Then I was standing for angry womankind herself, itself, bitchin' and moanin' about the injustice of the Body Politic being the body political.

Finally, I was standing for the notorious and sensationalistic La Luna madness of ovulating Abzug-ienne woman run wild.

I've stood for so many things this year I need to sit down a while and catch my breath.

What am I? The first person who's ever told a critic to fuck off? It ain't like they're elected to public office or have some public trust thing happening. So I sent the little cocksucker some faxes. Big deal.

I wrote a POME for
my friends at ABC

Black Eye

Why business with idiots and carnivorous carnival freaks whose Hot eyes dark and dank roll around to disguise the flippy lips that jiggle like snakes?

Why choose this fetid burial ground for one to play where there lives nothing at all here but urge and moisture?

There are no poets here, only scribblers shitting out

the hothouse turd of the day for the befuddled bungholed masses hungry for news from the other side:

Where people are alive and God and justice prevail with a wave of the hand and the flick of a button by a boogered finger dripping peanut butter.

Lulled there by magicians and barkers who sell the elixir by the pound—sugared, steeled and japonesed. Oh, yes, ye mass markets and demographic wizards whose job it is to know know know and yes yes yes!

Go to It, Fine Sirs, in bustling skirts oopsy-daisy! You fine proud clucking cocksmen who've carved the controlled climate of the retailed cosmos!

Yes, I'll have yet another of your glasses of grog and be merry right along with you, plan and push and play plain and pretty. What fun, what ghastly fun you all have given to myself and the world inside me.

Not really poets, not really scribblers, no, you, the god-blessed salesman playing chess with yourself all day long alone for money.

THE
NAMELESS

*G*oing *from room to room. Atleast ten times a day*
you run from the people who love you because
they love you and you know love is the worst
thing they can give you.

Atleast ten times a day you need to sit in a locked
room, car, or bathroom and just be.

Atleast ten times a day you want to forget it, go
back and deny it, pretend, be part of it again.

Atleast ten times a day you want to hurt yourself in
some sinister way that compels you back to the darkness.

Atleast ten times a day you want to suck the life out
of everyone you love—to possess them in every possible

*way—to fight them for loving you, to punish them, push
them away, make them leave.*

*Atleast ten times a day you try to put yourself inside
other people's heads, and you lose yourself there.*

*Atleast ten times a day you try to excuse, forgive,
feel sorry for and believe your abusers. They lie so well,
sometimes you do believe it.*

*But then, atleast ten times a day, maybe twenty, you
remember their secret faces, words, and slaps and you
feel the puke and bile rising up from your stomach, the
cold chill, you remember how big they were and how
small you were.*

*Atleast ten times a day you have to remind yourself
that you have already lived through the worst of it and
survived. The great despair you feel is so close to the relief, the hatred so close to the peace.*

*The loneliness so close to the belief in God. The hol-
low and full run together.*

In September, Tom and I got a call from the Van
Nuys psych center, where my daughter Jess was a patient
(after we got sober, we made it a point to get the kids sober and taken care of). Her therapist explained that Jess
had something to tell us, something that had taken her
months to work up to.

Jess told us that on our wedding night, her grandfa-
ther—my father—had grabbed her breasts and her butt,
did it over and over again with a big smile on his face,
with my mother standing next to him. Hearing this, I
spent the next few hours vacillating between a roaring,
all-consuming hate, an *energy* of hate that could bring
life to petrified wood or burn it to blackness and
nothing—I mean nothing—and the inescapable desire to

become nothing, to swallow myself and disappear, to gnaw out the part of me that perceived, gave life, tasted, smelled, heard, conceived, touched, reasoned, worried, cried—howled. I was having my second detestable Epiphany, another trip through the culvert of time, time to relive all the dull horrors that suddenly sounded so decayingly similar to Jess's experience—provided by her grandfather/my father.

More rationalization, more dissembling, more reality-tinting (rose-colored is not always such a good hue), more denial, as when Stephanie called me in Denver, when Daddy put his hand down her pants.

I had said to her once, "Well, it's just like he always did, isn't it? It's no different from what he's done hundreds of times." Hundreds of times, hundreds of fears, hundreds of jolts, hundreds of lies. Hundreds of dads stretch out in front of their kids on the living room floor and play with their penises for hours while the family makes jokes about it: Hey, Dad, did you find anything good? Everyone's Dad sticks his hand down his daughters' pants, squeezes their tits, their ass, their legs. *Every* twelve-year-old gets photographed with a movie camera by her father while she's in the tub and *every* teenage girl has to put a washrag over the doorknob in the bathroom to keep her father from peeking in the keyhole while she's taking a bath, right? *All* fathers talk sexually all the time to their daughters, don't they? *All* mothers hold pillows over their children's faces until they black out or pretend to, and stare at their children with hatred-edged eyes. There were no boundaries.

I have had to learn to define boundaries, learn what's appropriate as an adult, but for a long time, I had no idea. There was no place to go where they couldn't get me, except into my own head.

So Tom immediately called my parents to confront them to end the secret on Jess's behalf. My mother, once again serving as my father's cardiologist, wouldn't allow us to speak with my father, fearing he'd suffer a heart attack, which, of course, was impossible. My mother had one big concern—How could we believe Jess?

"Why are you calling us?" my sisters and brother demanded when Tom finally got in touch with them.

"I'm calling you because your niece was molested by your father."

"Well, we don't believe it," they answered—all of them: Stephanie, Geraldine, and my brother, Ben. Evidently, Stephanie's memory was worse than mine. The reason she came to live with me in Denver, you will recall, was because my father had physically and sexually abused her. (She denied it later.)

While Tom filed police reports in three states, I had to talk to my daughter. "I have to tell you something, Jess," I started slowly. "He did it to me, too—a lot, when I was a kid. He did it to Steph, too."

Here's what Bill, Jess's natural father, had to say about it when Tom called him about the molestation:

"You believe her?"

"Well, yeah. Rosey and I both believe Jess. There's no reason for her to make a story like that up."

"I suppose . . . unless . . ."

"The hospital filed a state report before we even found out about it, Bill. She didn't get any help from us, okay?"

"Well, I gotta investigate the facts first," my wise, always circumspect ex-husband hedged. Then he went and resumed contact with my mother and father, commiserating with them. My parents were never big fans of Bill's. Not until a shitload of sewage began to appear on the still surface of their fucked-up piety. Suddenly, Bill was a fine parent. But how could any parent whose daughter said that she was molested by somebody remain friendly with that person? This is not a stranger, a friend of a friend, or even a friend—this is your daughter, for God's sake. At best, you'd keep your distance from those whom she's accused; at worst, you'd chase them down with a twelve-gauge. But be friends with them? NO, NO, NO. NO. "It's just the poor kid's word against his," Tom said. In the end, my father again escaped responsibility. We tried to file charges against him in Utah, in California, and in Idaho. So far, in almost four years, nothing has come of it.

In the beginning, my father hid behind definitions and terminologies, used them like a dressing room partition to hide his guilt. "How could it be incest? We never had sex. *I* never had sex." He thinks incest is only about penetration, putting the penis in the vagina—so does my mother and so do a lot of people. When I got interviewed by *People* magazine, the first thing they wanted to know was whether or not there was penetration. And with that, they put themselves in the company of my father, who, at that Barr family summit in Las Vegas years ago, negotiated the terms of his responsibility, plea-bargained for the term "molestation" instead of "incest." That he could live with, that he could accept. "I'll take molest. I can handle that," he told my sister in the hotel suite. See, if it's just molest, that's not too bad because any hysterical woman can call anything molestation.

The more I thought about my family, the less I was able to function on a daily basis. I wept, I challenged myself, I rode the back of my spirit with hand spurs. I blamed myself in ways that demoralized my very core, split me into thin, flimsy wafers. "They don't love me" kept sounding in my head, and that pain is unparalleled in this mortal world.

R E C O V E R Y

I decided to go public as an incest survivor in a speech to other survivors in Denver, September 1991. I had, as my mentor and friend, Marilyn Van Derber Atler, the former Miss America, speaker, advocate, and fellow incest survivor.

I have chosen to become a soldier in a terrible war against children, innocence, ultimately a war against ourselves. Being abused leaves a child with a whirlpool of self-hate, funneling down into numbness. You lose your ability to judge places and people. You no longer know who or what is safe. An abused child becomes a perpetual victim in situation after situation, time and time again.

Last year, over Christmas, I had an operation to have my flap-apron-gut-belly cut off, removed, reshaped. At first I was very nervous and a little ashamed about it—maybe embarrassed—I guess a good sign of recovery is being able to tell the difference between shame and embarrassment—which I'm beginning to do now.

My stomach has hung down, in a flap/fold over my genitals for most of my life that I can remember. From hip to hip, it looked like a rolled up beach towel attached to my middle. Losing weight decreased its size but still, it was always there. I heard John Bradshaw about three years ago on TV talk about incest/sexual abuse victims gaining lots of weight in order to unconsciously hide their genitalia. I have thought about that often. When I used to look at my naked self in the mirror, first I noticed my large, flat and pendulous breasts—distended and misshapen from gaining/losing/gaining/losing fifty, eighty, one hundred pounds every year. Next I would see my stomach. The shame I felt about my body made me feel I was unlovable, unacceptable and encouraged me to have degrading sex with unloving partners.

This body, which had always been the receptacle of violence and abuse, I abused further by inflicting tears, holes and gouges on my belly, breasts, buttocks, thighs, everywhere unseen. This, I later learned, is not uncommon among incest victims.

After my stomach operation, I walked nude into the bathroom when I turned the corner. I saw, right there in the mirror, my sexual parts. I froze, I felt shocked. I felt vulnerable and scared, without the hiding places I had created so far.

I feel that I have been able to reverse the years of damage to my physical being and my self-esteem. After forty-one years, I finally feel *no shame* or disgust looking at myself in a mirror—I am a big, round, normal-shaped woman, with scars. Sometimes I feel as if I've had cut away my own self-loathing and am finding comfort in my own skin.

POWER

"There are two kinds of power," says the author Starhawk. "One is power over, which is always destructive, and the other is power from within, which is a transcendent and creative power."

The problem for me, from the very beginning was that I needed to believe that my inner power belonged to everyone else. I thought myself only a trustee, saving the world.

Later, when the smoke cleared, I realized that it had just been myself I was really trying to save all along. It certainly seemed easier when I projected all that hot air into the giant life raft, the imaginary ark that would carry Womankind herself over the flood of helplessness and betrayal.

I knew I was destined to come to Hollywood—I had always had that idea—I knew what the message would be and I knew that the *medium was the message*! Thank you, Professor McLuhan.

I came to Hollywood to take over, to claim TV as the new preserve of Woman. I came as Atill-ess the Hun, because I was "sick of what they're saying and I'm going to tell the truth!"

TV is a language all its own, a land of one dimensional stereotypes that destroys culture, not adds to it. TV is anti-art, a reflection of consumerism that serves the power structure. TV is about demographics. Demographics are about women who buy products. Women have been made prisoners of TV—the more they watch, the more products they buy. Why, then, if TV is largely a medium for and about women, are most of the women on TV being raped, murdered, humiliated, degraded, reduced to their body parts and verbally attacked? The more power we are told we don't have, the more power we're willing to concede.

In *my* show, the Woman is no longer a victim, but in control of her own mind. I wanted to make family sitcoms as we know them obsolete.

I wanted to make television that is not a tool of cor-

porate America, television that is instead in direct oppo-
sition to corporate thinking altogether.

The "Roseanne" show is a show about America's
unwashed unconscious. Every episode sprouts at least a
seed of something banal turned on its ass, something so
pointedly "incorrect," filtered through a working class
language that claims every MALE-defined thing from
family to economics, to God, as belonging, rightfully, and
at last, to the realm of women.

I became a fighter, a soldier, in 1980. I wanted to
bring to the stage, to the media, to the arts, and *to my
own life*, the idea of a woman who was strong and brave,
sly and mouthy.

I created a television show called "Roseanne," which
became the battleground of and for myself. To allow for
the freedom, the creative control, and the growth of this
show, I had to become as strong, brave, sly, and mouthy
as that woman on TV.

Many people have written me to say that they have
been inspired by the stories, the family dynamics, and the
honesty of this show. No one has been as inspired by it
as *me*.

Because of the success of this show, I have been
given the incredible opportunity to turn my life around.
To get up when I was headed down. I almost did go
down for good when they gave men the credit for my
work, degraded me for being successful while rewarding
my male friends for doing the same, called me a liar when

I told the truth, attacked my husband as a charlatan—for loving me.

But I didn't go down after all, because the men and women inside me refused to let me, and, surrounding me, they yanked me forward and in, back to them.

I belong away from that world of snakes and carnival barkers, that world of cynicism and bitterness that walls out the light of Heaven and tunnels it into a channel that can be switched off and darkened.

I cared the most.

TO MY KIDS

I'm sorry:

I'm sorry for the time lost in haste and worry and practice for a place that would later never be.

I'm sorry for the times when I could not make my arms available to you, afraid of the damage they might do since they seemed not to be mine.

I'm sorry I wasn't there so much of the time I gave you. So many me's would answer back at you across the river I could not swim.

I'm sorry for the times of violence from my own mouth and from my hands that hardened those soft places you held sacred.

I'm sorry for leaving you in unsafe places—I did not

know where the ground was broken, and stepping over those fissures was all my life. I did not want to know. I could not bear to know.

I'm sorry for the trademark of stories I brought you, a hand-me-down quilt of memories that transcend speech, or lie just below, uncovered, shivering, naked, circled by genealogical buzzards diving and swooping overhead waiting to succor the rot left to me and passed to you.

God, freeze the family hands, lips, the thousand diseases of us this time, in this generation.

Spare me my grandchildren—as you have spared me.

MY LIVES

This book has been such an ordeal for me to write, I oughta write a book about it.

To tell these stories and try to go back and do the piecework of time, which has always eluded me anyway has cost me so much unmitigated pain, that on this night, I just cannot bear it in any way.

Many nights, I have lain awake, just pounding the air with my own breath, fists clenched, begging God for the serenity to sleep or to feel eased at all.

Many mornings, I have awakened to find bloody

holes torn in my groin and thighs. I kept cutting my fingernails shorter and shorter.

But nothing has stopped me; not gloves, not clothing, not psychoanalysis, including one brief hospitalization (upon finding myself in Barston, California, in my car, having forgotten how to drive, and thinking only of going to the parents' house in Salt Lake City to corner, contain, frighten, and shut them up).

I set out to write a book about surviving incest and abuse. I so very much wanted to write a happy and inspiring story. Tonight, again, I know there is no happy or inspiring ending to any of this. Only that I lived through it, and that in spite of its hovering and crushing weight, just the reality of it, just the possession of my body and mind and soul in its aftermath, somehow, I, like millions of others, carried on.

The carrying on seems to mean nothing most days. There simply is nothing else to do.

Somedays I feel as though I have lost too much, and nothing will make it better. Nothing at all, not drugs, not alcohol, not even speaking out as an advocate, not therapy, not writing, just nothing. Nothing.

I survived my childhood by birthing many separate identities to stand in for one another in times of great stress and fear. Each one was created to do only one thing.

Every day is a struggle to remember, to hold on, to choose to live. I am an overweight overachiever with a few dandy compulsive-obsessive disorders and a little problem with self-mutilation. No, no, no—money doesn't make it better, nor success, nor even a happy marriage.

Every day I teeter on the edge of a razor blade. If things get too bad, I go away and someone else comes in and tidies up the humble abode of my mind. That person stays until someone else is needed.

My husband and children have gone half mad over my absences and, at times, my forgetting their names, their ages and whose mother is whose.

You don't understand. Perhaps you don't want to—or simply can't. There is no scarier chasm of darkness than the human mind.

Being "many" has given me my life. It is a basic correction in evolution that needed to be made to allow for my survival. I will not discuss my therapy on TV or while selling this book, but I wanted to tell the truth, especially to all those of you out there who already know it, and find yourself in strange places using unfamiliar names having forgotten what happened to you, leaning closer and closer over the abyss.

This is how we survive—cut off from our own parts, severed arteries of memory, time, connection. Like vampires and night creatures, we wander the earth, alone, haunted, not owning a body, just temporarily inhabiting one. Crazy all the way.

Not funny, neurotic crazy, but bloodshot eyes,

looking into mirrors, not recognizing what looks back. Crazy. Dead.

How many of us are there? Shall we choose to march, to make ourselves and our numbers visible? How many times would we ring the world?

I wish I could take away your pain, and mine. I can't. Hiding under stairs, disassociating, running away, getting help to face it—all of these ways of just coping have failed, except in the smallest of terms.

The sneering smugness of my family of origin revolts me, even though I know the truth of their victimization, too. I am so impotent I cannot even hate them—they are too sad.

This, then, is the end of this book. I went through a four-year-long trauma to write it; reading and rereading certain parts caused me to remember still more terrors. I want to put this in the past and move on now.

Am I getting well?

I just know that so far I have met many people who share my body. I am grateful to them all for saving my life:

2
Baby
Cindy
Susan
Nobody
Somebody

Joey
Heather
Roger
Kevin
Evangelina
Vangie
Martha
Mother
Piggy
Fucker
Bambi
Rosey
Roseanne
ONE

The day of my childhood happy and red
snaked up on me
from behind
as I, bandaged and prone, began
calling
for forgiveness
and names to quiet the shellings
of brick and dirt tenements of
memory.

I remembered the mailboxes, black iron
with lock ports being undug
and rehung by men in white
canvas paintings on a frilly
wooden post
now split in half and de-scrivelered

Then the painted, faded, redded porch gave way
to concrete
and flower boxes to steel, while
apricots and roses
bloomed and fell and machines ate grass with
sawing motion
that left the jagged smell
dancing and sizzling
up from the ground
while

white and yellow puffers' heads torn off
flew straight up, and ran
like shots from a gun.

Me, peeking from around where dirt became
rock, and then, something
harder
Red-nosed and nasty, smirking in stolen
breaths while I watched
fairies and Parrots
Entertwine
As the shadows crept from under the
house and spilled out, along the grass
into the street, soaking its hedges.

I hovered over the little sidewalk that led to an
arbor of purple grapes and green leaves crunching
Entwisted on an arch
That might have been mirrored—
The blue of God's
heavenly eye
so vivid that day; just for me,
a young girl in
corduroy overalls and black mushroom hair.

And Rounding the Cellar Door that
slanted
padlocked in soft brown
earth

Where the Green Gilled Mother Hen grew
                    with her cabbaged leaf
          babies
               Round and Round
conversing with staining marigolds
Beneath the window of the Grandmother's
               laced creaked curtaining
                    window
and next to the window where the uncle
                    slept before he married
I charted Barbed wire and crickets
                    beyond
mapping field after green field
                    that
               Cradled rounder cars
               and
               Square boxes
                    traversed by
wayfaring fattened kitty cats
                    Fluffed by the rain
uncovering themselves with a lick
               and a dart and a jump
               testing for clear weather

Above the Birds, hopping on telephone wires
     like proud soldiers, blue uniformed
tapping out their Morse codes:
          Land below!

Mates and Bread Crumbs
too
from the Grandmother who
owned the House and the Apron

Full of dried Friday night
bread, who gave it to me, to
stuff in my pockets to
Feed The Birds
(and myself a mouthful when the birds looked
away).

Everywhere Dusk, Dogs Arguing
and the smell of things
Dying and Growing
souring sweetly with
the days'
photosynthesis

This, my yard, my village, my tiny
Queendom
where I danced and Pirated and
dreamed and jumped
unscrubbed and twirling
Soon to be freckled and ponytailed

Oh, yes, That Day—

I saw the changes of all the seasons roll out and
away
The cars—
  first covered in snow then rust
The sheds—
  first white then gray then wooden
        splintered
The lawn—
    gone brown and covered in stubble
      grown to rocks that crunched
        at first underfoot
        when newly poured
    trapped later in muddy murk below
    the earth like flattened candy bar
      wrappers—

and I remembered then, how each day had
proceeded a day before it.
          and how
  each
        continued, followed by
        another—
        Time
Unbroken time—connected to itself over
and over and over until the
        41st Year